W9-CFB-812

Diana & Dodi

A LOVE STORY

For information:

Tallfellow Press, Inc.
1180 South Beverly Drive, Suite 320
Los Angeles, CA 90035

Distributed by General Publishing Group, Los Angeles

Library of Congress Cataloging-in-Publication Data

Delorm, Rene.
Diana & Dodi : a love story / by Rene Delorm with Barry Fox and Nadine Taylor.
p. cm.
ISBN 1-57544-113-6
1. Diana, Princess of Wales, 1961–1997 . 2. Princesses—Great Britain—Biography. 3. Al Fayed, Dodi. I. Fox, Barry. II. Taylor, Nadine. III. Title.
DA591.A45D531324 1998
941.085'092—dc21
[b] 98-29043
CIP

Printed in the USA by RR Donnelley & Sons Company
10 9 8 7 6 5 4 3 2

Tallfellow Press
Los Angeles

A LOVE STORY

BY RENE DELORM

WITH BARRY FOX AND NADINE TAYLOR

Dedicated to Prince William, Prince Harry
and Mr. Mohammed Al Fayed.

ACKNOWLEDGMENTS

Thanks to Barry and Nadine, for their sensitivity and skill in helping me put my thoughts and my story on paper; to Larry Sloan and Leonard Stern of Tallfellow Press, who provided insightful and much appreciated guidance, and without whom this book would not have been published in the United States and Canada; to Chuck Hurewitz, for his patience, advice and belief in the book; to Heide Lange, who lovingly shepherded the project from beginning to end; to Amel and her son, for being in my life; and to David Rosen, for making me realize how important it was to write this book.

Finally, thanks to my two sons, Alain and Bruno, for their unwavering support. Wherever life leads, you will always have my deepest respect, support and love.

TABLE OF CONTENTS

PROLOGUE

The Last Night

Twilight spread slowly over Paris, the beautiful City of Lights, on the evening of August 30, 1997. As dusk approached, the city's many famous sights—the Eiffel Tower, Arc de Triomphe, Sacré-Coeur and Notre-Dame—were dramatically highlighted by floodlights, emphasizing their magnificence and giving the city a glamour and mystery unmatched anywhere in the world. Despite living in Paris for three years, I never tired of watching the city transform itself from a bustling metropolis by day into a glowing jewel by night.

Dressed in my butler's "night uniform" of black pants, white shirt, black vest and black bow tie, I sat in my quarters, feeling as listless and inert as the night air. I was awaiting word from my boss, Dodi Fayed, that it was time to serve cocktails and hors d'oeuvres to him and his new love, Diana, Princess of Wales. The two of them were getting ready for a night on the town—their last together for a while because she would be returning to London the following day. But I knew there would be many more to come, because they were madly in love with each other. Of that I was absolutely certain. You see, I had been lucky enough to witness the birth and blossoming of their entire love affair, from first bud to full bloom.

I was tired from the day's activities—just that morning we had returned from a nine-day stay on the *Jonikal*, the Fayed family's fabulous yacht. This was the second cruise we had all taken in a month's time, the first one lasting seven days, and in between I had served my boss and the princess at three different Fayed family homes—one in London, one in the English countryside and, of course, here at our home base in Paris. We had flown to Nice twice and visited Monte Carlo, Portofino, the island of Corsica and the ritzy resort of Cala di Volpe on the island of Sardinia, all in a month's time. No wonder I was tired!

We had also been chased and photographed endlessly on land and sea by paparazzi, pursued doggedly on foot, on motorcycles, in cars and in boats. Their pictures, some taken up close, but the majority through telephoto lenses, had been splashed across the pages of newspapers worldwide. And there was every indication that this media frenzy wasn't about to die down anytime soon. In fact, at that very moment a pack of paparazzi was lurking outside the front door of our building.

I sat there in my easy chair reminding myself that soon after I served the hors d'oeuvres, I would be left alone for several hours. Then I'd be able to finish my unpacking, relax and maybe even doze a little before they returned. At last I'd have some quiet time, time to wind down.

Just then, I heard my boss open the far door to the kitchen. Jumping from my chair, I walked swiftly through the door that connected my quarters to the kitchen, intercepting him just as he stepped through the doorway. The harassed and angry feelings that had claimed him an hour earlier as he fought his way through the paparazzi had melted away and on his face was a look of pure joy and happiness. Seeing me, he put his finger to his lips and motioned for me to come closer, wearing the excited look of a child on Christmas morning. He obviously had some wonderful secret to tell.

"Rene," he whispered, his eyes gleaming, "make sure we have champagne on ice when we come back from dinner. I'm going to propose to her tonight!"

I looked at him, too stunned to speak. Although I'd imagined that one day he and the princess might get married, never in my wildest dreams had I thought it would happen this fast!

My jaw dropped, and all I could choke out was, "Really?" Dodi laughed at my shocked expression.

Recovering a little bit, I added, "I mean, that's absolutely fantastic! She is just wonderful, Mr. Fayed, and I know you'll be very, very happy!"

I truly meant it. The princess was one of the nicest, most down-to-earth people I had ever met, and she certainly had a good effect on my boss. In the seven years

I had worked for Dodi Fayed I had never seen him this happy. I was just shocked at how quickly things had progressed.

He grinned at me as if he would burst with joy. Then, glancing behind him to make sure the princess was nowhere in sight, he produced a small, light gray velvet box from the famous jeweler, Alberto Repossi.

"Look at this," he whispered, as he carefully raised the lid. There, embedded in the white satin lining, was a spectacular, diamond-encrusted ring—a massive stone surrounded by clusters of diamonds, set on a yellow-and-white gold band. Later, I would learn that it was worth more than two hundred thousand dollars.

"What do you think?" Dodi asked.

Looking at that spectacular ring, I could summon up only one word.

"Wow!" I breathed reverently.

I looked back at his face, and all I could think was what a long way he had come. I used to say to him, "Mr. Fayed, why don't you get married, settle down and have some kids?" His reply was always an emphatic "Never!" He had been married once in 1987 to a beautiful model, Suzanne Gregard, but they had parted after only ten months and he seemed dead set against marriage ever since.

"No more," he would tell me. "No marriage, no kids. I want to stay single and enjoy my life."

Yet now he stood before me, thrilled to his fingertips, announcing his intention to propose to the princess after a whirlwind six-week love affair. Who could have imagined it?

"Mr. Fayed," I told him sincerely, "I am so very happy for you and for the princess. This is a wonderful, wonderful night."

"Yes." he replied, as he carefully closed the ring box and pocketed it. "Tonight will top everything. So make sure you have the champagne ready. We'll be back around midnight."

CHAPTER 1

Meeting Dodi

I was a very young boy when I first fell in love—but it wasn't with a woman, it was with American movies. What made this rather unusual was that I spent the first nineteen years of my life in Morocco, a French protectorate located on the northwest coast of Africa, across the Strait of Gibraltar from Spain. I was born there in 1943 and grew up in a community of Arabs, French, Berbers, Spaniards, Jews and others. In the streets I would hear the languages of all of those people, but I spoke only French and a little bit of "street" Arabic. Yet I managed to watch as many American movies as possible, since they came to the local movie house dubbed in French.

Being both Jewish and fatherless (my parents divorced before I was born), life was not exactly easy. We had very little money and few creature comforts—no refrigerator, no telephone, no television—but my mother did manage to scrape together enough to send me to the movies regularly. There I could escape into a world of fantasy and magic. Ninety percent of the films that came to Morocco were American, so I grew up loving America and all things American.

At nineteen, I was drafted into the French Army for a two-year stint. Meanwhile, my family moved to Canada. Once out of the service I ended up following them, settling in Montreal, in the "French" part of Canada. I was amazed at the sights, sounds and smells of the big city, having seen very little of the world up to that point. I got a job as a waiter in a discotheque and soon met the woman who would become my wife.

I first laid eyes on Christine when she came to the disco with a date. She was stunningly beautiful; what a face, what a body! I couldn't stop staring at her. Surprisingly, she couldn't stop staring at me either. We made eye contact many times throughout the evening. When her date excused himself to go to the restroom, I had to make my move. He left the table for five minutes; I got her phone number and married her!

We had two sons, Alain and Bruno, living quite happily in Montreal for ten years. Then it gradually dawned on me that it was *cold* in Canada (it took me only ten years to come to this realization!), so I decided to move to California, where the climate was more like that of Morocco. There was just one catch—I could barely speak English. But when you're young, you think you can do anything. So, full of optimism and hope, I packed up my young family and made the trek to beautiful, sunny Los Angeles.

After a brief stint working in a pizzeria, I landed a job as a waiter at L'Auberge, a popular French restaurant on the Sunset Strip. Despite my almost nonexistent English, the owner gave me a chance to serve just one table; he was breaking me in a little at a time. I learned to recite the menu and the specials in passable English, but if a customer asked me a question about the food, I was in trouble. My language blunders were sometimes hilarious and always embarrassing.

One day, while reciting the list of specials, I said, "Today we have a wonderful baby dog served with orange and steamed vegetables."

Horrified, the couple looked at each other.

"Baby dog?" the man asked incredulously.

"Yes," I replied quizzically.

"I didn't know they ate dogs in France," the woman gasped.

"Oh, yes," I replied. "Is a great specialty in France. Is served with orange and sometimes fruit. We call it Dog à L'Orange."

"Ohhhh," said the woman, suddenly getting it. "He means *duck*." A look of relief passed over both their faces before they began to laugh uproariously.

"What did I say?" I asked, surprised.

"You said *dog*," the woman replied, laughing as though her sides would split. "You know, 'ruff ruff.' You meant *duck*, 'quack quack.'"

Fortunately, my butchering of the English language seemed to amuse most of my customers, so I was given more and more tables to wait on.

Once my English had improved a bit, I decided to try to move up in the world. (Christine and I had recently separated, so a new job would provide a much-needed lift. We loved each other, but were simply incompatible.) I applied for a job at the ritzy Ma Maison restaurant on Melrose Avenue in West Hollywood, home of the famous chef Wolfgang Puck. With its beautiful gardenlike atmosphere and superb food, it had the reputation of being one of the finest restaurants in the city. And it had caught the fancy of the show business crowd, which made it even more appealing to me, the old movie buff.

Luck was with me; I got the job, and once I started working at Ma Maison, I felt I'd undergone a metamorphosis. One day I was just a waiter who spoke bad English, the next I was serving many of the great movie stars I had seen on the screen as a boy in Morocco. Some days I could hardly believe it! Eventually, I even remarried, completing my happiness.

My very first customer was a famous attorney who had a reputation for being difficult to please. He always insisted on immediate service, and if he didn't get it, he was quite capable of making a scene. In fact, most of the other waiters were afraid of him. One day he came in at a very busy time and his waiter couldn't get to him immediately, so Ma Maison's owner, Patrick Terrail, asked me to take his drink order.

Somewhat hesitantly, I approached the attorney's table, greeted him and asked if I could bring any cocktails. I had enough command of the language to handle that much smoothly. But when I returned with the drinks, to my horror he asked me about the specials. I desperately looked over at Patrick, hoping he would rescue me, but he just smiled. He wanted to see how well I would do. So, taking a deep breath, I began to stumble my way through the specials. I was extremely nervous and, to make matters worse, I began to stutter, making my poor English even more incomprehensible. But he just smiled encouragingly and waited for me to finish. Then he turned to Patrick and said with a laugh, "This guy reminds me of Charles Boyer" (the great French actor).

As I returned to the kitchen, wiping the sweat off my brow, Patrick patted me on the back and said, "From now on he's yours." After that, I waited on the supposedly difficult attorney every time he came in and he always treated me extremely well.

I worked at Ma Maison for close to eight years, but I had the most fun during the last three when I was "promoted" to the VIP section, where the celebrities were always seated. Many of the other waiters didn't want to work this section, for it could be very stressful. These people were used to getting instant service and a great deal of attention, and many would get unpleasant if everything didn't go exactly the way they wanted. But for some reason I didn't have much trouble with celebrities; in fact, I was almost always able to please them, partly because I was fast and had developed a knack for anticipating their needs. I actually enjoyed waiting on them, not to mention the big tips they'd leave and the outside jobs they sometimes offered me.

Ed McMahon, Johnny Carson's famous sidekick on *The Tonight Show,* was one of my regulars. A very friendly man, he was one of the customers who hired me for an outside job. He pulled me aside one day and said, "Rene, I need you for a very special event. But it's got to be a big secret."

"Sir," I answered, "it will be a great privilege."

A few days later, at the appointed time, Patrick Terrail and I went to the construction site of the McMahons' new home-to-be in Beverly Hills. The foundation had been poured and the frame was in place, but that was about it—no ceiling, walls, plumbing or electricity. There was, however, plenty of mud and slosh. Patrick and I examined the unusual setting before finding just the right place. We laid out a little carpet, set up a dinner table, lit candles and hung a painting on what would one day become a wall. Soon a chef arrived, set up a portable kitchen and began to prepare the food.

It was still light when the McMahons drove by, supposedly on their way to dinner at Ma Maison. As Victoria McMahon later told me, her husband had said, "Honey, before we go to the restaurant, I'd like to show you how far the house has progressed."

"No," she protested. "I'm all dressed. It's too muddy there."

But he insisted, so they pulled up to the house, stepped carefully through the mud that would become the front yard and went inside. Mr. McMahon showed her the living room and then took her to the dining room. As they entered, she caught sight of the table set for dinner, candles lighted, and me ready to serve them.

"Surprise!" shouted Mr. McMahon, with his unmistakable, jovial laugh.

Mrs. McMahon couldn't believe it. "We're having dinner here?"

Looking at the wine and appetizers, all neatly set out, she laughed, "Rene, you were a part of this!" and gave me a hug.

Times like that made my job and my life extra special. So did the occasions on which a VIP took the time to assist me.

One of my regular customers was the great actor, director and writer, Orson Welles. One day I was feeling very down and, although I always tried to keep my personal problems to myself, Mr. Welles detected my mood.

He said, "Rene, what's wrong?"

"Sir?" I said, surprised.

"I see in your eyes that something is troubling you."

"Oh. Well," I replied, not wanting to impose on him but feeling the need to talk, "I'm separating from my wife, Brenda. It's all my fault, she's a wonderful girl. My kids love her, but I guess I wasn't ready for a second marriage."

I had met Brenda in 1981 while she was working as a waitress at the Moustache Cafe on Melrose Avenue near Ma Maison. I often went there to eat, and one day she happened to be my waitress. She won my heart with her first smile, and eight months later we were married. Born in the Midwest, she was pretty, funny, exciting and down to earth. Unfortunately, I was simply not prepared to marry again. My two sons were especially disappointed when Brenda and I separated, for they had grown very fond of their stepmother.

A few days after my conversation with Mr. Welles, my soon-to-be ex-wife called.

"Rene," she said, "I have in front of me a beautiful bouquet of flowers and a letter from Orson Welles. It says, 'Dear Brenda, Rene is a good friend of mine. He feels so guilty'...and on and on and on."

I couldn't believe that Mr. Welles had done that for me! The next time I saw him I thanked him profusely, but he only wanted to know if it had helped. And it did, for it brought us back together, if only temporarily.

One of Ma Maison's biggest attractions was its extraordinarily talented chef, Wolfgang Puck. But toward the end of my tenure at the restaurant, Wolfgang began to get restless. He quit Ma Maison, wrote a best-selling cookbook and opened his own restaurant, Spago, above the Sunset Strip.

Spago had a wonderful, modern, airy decor centered around an open kitchen that allowed guests to watch the master at work. It quickly became *the* place to see and be seen. After Spago had been open for about a year, Wolfgang asked me to join his staff. I went willingly. After only six months, I again became the VIP waiter, serving such stars as Robert De Niro, Bob Hope, Jimmy Stewart, Suzanne Pleshette, Phil Collins, Elizabeth Taylor, Richard Burton, Clint Eastwood, Oliver Stone, Magic Johnson, Sean Connery and Jackie Collins.

Robin Leach, host of *Lifestyles of the Rich & Famous*, was one of my favorites. Once, when I was off work, I went into Spago with a date for a drink. Robin was there, throwing a party. He insisted that we join his gathering, sitting us down at a table and getting the waiter to take our order. That was a great feeling, being served in the place where I usually served others!

Supermogul Michael Ovitz, who was then head of CAA, the most powerful talent agency in Hollywood, was also one of my regulars. In fact, whenever he used Spago to cater a dinner party at his home, he requested that I be there to serve. On a couple of occasions, he had very special guests with whom he was engaged in delicate negotiations. His wife, Judy, impressed upon me the importance of these deals and the need for absolute secrecy. Mr. Ovitz went one step further.

"Rene," he said, "when it comes time to serve, I want *you* to be the only person coming into this room."

So three or four people would bring food from the kitchen to the closed dining room door. From there, I would take the plates into the room and serve. It was a little hectic, having to serve food and drinks to ten or more people by myself, but it was well worth the effort. In addition to signing for the twenty-five percent service fee, Mr. Ovitz would later send me an extra tip and a personal note of thanks. I still have those notes; they mean a great deal to me.

One time Mr. Ovitz brought Steven Spielberg, Michael Crichton and several other guests to the restaurant, where they sat at a table festooned with dinosaur decorations to celebrate their upcoming movie, *Jurassic Park*. My teenage son, Bruno, wanted to be a director one day and, like everyone else, was very impressed with Steven Spielberg's work. I didn't know the great director, so I asked Mr. Ovitz if it would be possible to get an autograph for my son. He gave the OK.

With a smile, Mr. Spielberg took a Spago menu and wrote, "To Bruno: Learn story before camera. Welcome to the movie world!"

As if that weren't enough, Mr. Ovitz later asked me if Bruno would like to meet Steven Spielberg personally.

"Are you kidding?" I almost shouted in reply. "It would be his dream!"

And so my son had the great privilege of meeting Steven Spielberg on the set of his movie, *Hook*, where he spent a few minutes chatting with Bruno and then arranged for him to take a three-hour tour of the set. Bruno was in heaven, and I was really touched by the great director's generosity. Yes, working at Spago did bring me some perks!

It's hard to think of Spago without remembering the star-studded Academy Awards parties that were hosted there for so many years by old-time Hollywood agent "Swifty" Lazar. This was an "A-list" party, *the* party for the show biz crowd, and everyone who was anyone wanted to be there. I worked at seven of them, always dressed in a tuxedo, happily witnessing one of the most exciting Hollywood events of the year.

The party was held in two "shifts." During the first shift, from six to nine-thirty, we served dinner while the invited guests watched the Academy Awards show on television. Then, everybody left to make way for the crowd coming directly from the Oscar ceremony itself. During this second "shift," we served appetizers and drinks, nothing elaborate, but the air was electric with excitement. Everybody was there—winners, losers and just about any big name you could think of.

In 1988, Swifty Lazar had the tables decorated with miniature Academy Award statuettes, complete with plaques that read: *60th Annual Academy Awards, Irving and Mary Lazar Party, April 11, 1988 at Spago*. I really wanted to take one home for a souvenir, but I knew, of course, I'd have to ask first. I finally summoned the courage to approach Mr. Lazar, who was just getting ready to leave.

"Excuse me, Mr. Lazar," I said humbly, "but I was wondering if you would mind if I took one of the statues home for a souvenir?"

The old man peered at me through his thick glasses and then a smile crinkled his face.

"Of course, Rene," he said, picking one up and handing it to me. "I was going to give you one anyway. You deserve an award after waiting on all those people!"

I still have it, sitting proudly on my bookshelf.

But the most exciting thing that happened to me during those years was being asked to appear in a movie—portraying what else? A maitre d'. One of my regular customers was Robert Towne, who wrote the screenplay for *Chinatown* and many other great movies. He was making a movie called *Tequila Sunrise*, starring Mel Gibson, Michelle Pfeiffer and Kurt Russell, and needed an Italian-looking maitre d'. "You'd be perfect," he told me, "you have an Italian look." The next thing I knew, I had my own trailer with my name on the door, and I was an actor in a Hollywood movie. It was so incredible to me: The little boy from Morocco who had fallen in love with America by watching its movies, was now in one himself.

One of my "methods" of taking special care of the VIPs was to check the reservation book in advance to see who was coming in, and have their drinks waiting for them on the table when they arrived. I was taking care of the same people over and over again, and most of them ordered the same cocktail each time. It was an easy way to put them in a good frame of mind. I never had a single customer who didn't appreciate the courtesy.

So I did the same thing for Mr. Dodi Fayed after he had come in a few times, and eventually it brought me more than just appreciation—it brought me a new way of life!

Emad "Dodi" Fayed was the son of the multimillionaire Mohammed Al Fayed, an Egyptian businessman who currently owns the legendary Harrods department store in London, the celebrated Hotel Ritz in Paris, Turnbull & Asser (a famous British shirtmaking company) and several magnificent residences in England and France. Born in Alexandria, Egypt, Dodi* was an only child and led a privileged but lonely life. His parents divorced when he was two and he remained with his father, whose growing shipping business forced him to be away much of the time. He attended Alexandria's finest private school, an institution emphasizing obedience and harsh discipline.

* Although I refer to my boss throughout the book as "Dodi" for simplicity's sake, I never called him by this name. It was *always* "Mr. Fayed."

At the age of fourteen, Dodi was enrolled in an expensive Swiss boarding school, where he rubbed shoulders with the children of movie stars and began to develop a lifelong interest in the film business. Meanwhile, his father, an avowed Anglophile, moved permanently to England, and a few years later Dodi enrolled at Britain's Royal Military Academy, Sandhurst. Neither would ever live in Egypt again.

Although Dodi had a chance to join the United Arab Emirates Air Force, he decided instead to become a movie producer and, backed by his father, set up Allied Stars, Ltd. in 1979. This production company eventually produced several movies, including *Breaking Glass*, *Chariots of Fire* (which won the Oscar for Best Picture of 1981) and *F/X*, while Dodi also received producing credit on *Hook* and *The Scarlet Letter*. In 1990, when I met him, *Hook* was in production and he was a member of the board of directors at both Harrods and Turnbull & Asser—a busy man indeed. Because he divided his time between Los Angeles and Europe, he didn't yet have a house in L.A., staying instead in a suite at the Hotel Bel Air.

When I met Dodi he was a confirmed bachelor, having been married once for just under a year. His ex-wife, Suzanne Gregard, was a striking, blond model who continued her career after the marriage. Unfortunately, her many absences, coupled with her dislike for Dodi's ever-present bodyguards, contributed to the demise of the marriage.

After Dodi had come into Spago a few times, I noticed that he always had an extra-dry vodka martini with an olive, or sometimes an onion. The first time I had his drink waiting for him, he thought there was some mistake. Looking around, he caught sight of me standing nearby, smiling.

"Hi, Mr. Fayed," I said, with a twinkle in my eye.

He indicated the drink. "That is for me?" he asked, surprised.

"Yes, sir."

"How did you know?"

"I remembered from last time."

From that moment on, I always took care of him. He was not a demanding person at all. He would order a little pizza to share with his guests while they enjoyed their cocktails. He was never in a hurry; whenever I was ready it was fine with him. I found him very, very pleasant to wait on, always extremely polite and a very generous tipper.

After coming in for a couple of months, he said, "Rene, I'm going to be moving permanently to California and I would like someone to take care of my parties and organize the things in my house. I would like you to do this, if you are interested."

I was very flattered. I had never imagined myself working for just one person. But knowing how kind, polite and respectful Dodi Fayed had always been, I was willing to consider it.

"Well, let's talk," I said, leaving it open-ended.

"How about in a couple of days in my suite at the Bel Air? That's where I live."

We had our meeting, and by then I'd had plenty of time to think it over.

"Mr. Fayed," I began, "here is what I can do for you: I can take care of your parties, your dinners and coordinating things at your home. I am not romantically attached to anyone, so I can travel with you whenever you need. I am also a personal trainer and a masseur. I can give you a full workout and massage afterwards. I don't smoke, drink or use drugs."

After a beat, I added hastily, "Also, I am Jewish," thinking that this might bother him because he was Egyptian and a Muslim.

To all of this, Dodi Fayed had but one thing to say: "That's perfect."

I was hired in June of 1990 and started a completely new phase of my life, working at a big, beautiful house that Dodi had just moved into on Beverly Drive in Beverly Hills. For me, it was the beginning of a great new adventure.

CHAPTER

2

Life With Dodi

When I first began working for Dodi I was primarily an entertainment director, not a butler. He usually had three or four parties a week, for which I would set up the tables, arrange the flowers, order the food and oversee the cleanup. (If Dodi was eating alone or with only one guest, I would often cook the dinner myself.) Once the guests arrived, I put on the music, served cocktails and appetizers, then dinner. For bigger parties, I was in charge of renting a large tent, silver service, plates, tables, flowers and table settings. I also hired musicians, chefs, extra waiters and any other personnel we might need.

In addition to my entertainment duties, I eventually began serving as a household manager, helping to supervise the maids and relaying instructions from Dodi to other employees, since he usually didn't like to confront people directly. My hours were great. Typically I started work at five in the afternoon, remaining at the house until Dodi went to bed, which meant that I had my days free. If it was very late when the evening ended, I was welcome to spend the night in a room that had been set aside for me. I did this about twice a week.

On an average day, arriving around five, I'd go to my room and get dressed in my uniform, then report to my boss to find out what was going on that evening (if I didn't already know). Although he often had guests, many nights he was alone and would cook certain Middle Eastern dishes that he remembered from childhood. He taught me how to make them and I recall our little cooking escapades with fondness. There would be just the two of us in the kitchen, because by then everybody else (the housekeeper, the maid, the secretary) would be gone.

Dodi would say, "Rene, we're going to cook the okra." Then he would hustle around the kitchen, pulling together ingredients, asking me to get certain bowls, pans or utensils, and we'd start to cook.

"Rene," he'd command, "take notes. Then when I tell you I want this dish, you will know how to make it."

He got a lot of pleasure out of cooking; it was fun for him. And as he cooked, he liked to bark out the orders: "Rene, garlic! Rene, paprika! Rene, cumin!"

When the ingredients had all been mixed together and a wonderful, exotic aroma began to permeate the atmosphere, Dodi would say, "OK, Rene, leave it there for another half hour or so. I will eat it tonight in the study."

Dodi also taught me how to make the best barbecue sauce in the world. One day, not too long after I began working for him, he said excitedly, "Rene, let me show you how to make the sauce for the spareribs." Then he asked me to bring several ingredients, including ketchup, paprika, garlic, cumin and a bottle of beer. I thought he was going to drink the beer while mixing the sauce, but instead he left it alone until everything else had been blended, shaken and stirred together. Then, picking up the bottle of beer, he said, "This is the secret ingredient." With that, he poured half the bottle into the sauce and offered me a taste. He was right; it was excellent. Whenever I barbecued for Dodi, which was quite often, we used that sauce.

But I was most impressed with the culinary magic he performed on eggplant (which he called *aubergine,* its French name). I was unconvinced that this vegetable could be made appetizing, but he showed me how to slice it, grill it well, add seasonings, lemon juice, garlic and other ingredients, then puree it. The result was scrumptious.

When he was alone, he often dined in his study. At around nine-thirty or ten, I'd serve his dinner and he would eat while talking on the phone or watching TV or videos. Sometimes he would cook his own dinner. He often prepared navy beans, to which he added chopped onions, garlic, cumin and several other spices. He loved to cook, to be creative and explore ways to mix flavors. My "day" usually ended around midnight, when Dodi would say, "OK, Rene, you can go home."

Sometimes, however, there would be one last chore. Before I left, he would ask me to put some bowls of water in the bedroom for his dogs, Romeo, a giant black schnauzer, and Shoe, a miniature gray schnauzer.

With a smile I would say, "Oh, is this the Ritz night?"

It was our private joke. The dogs normally slept in another room in the house, but sometimes Dodi let them sleep with him in his large, sumptuous, bedroom. It was like the Hotel Ritz, although there was always a price to pay. Romeo, who was huge, didn't just sleep quietly on the bed all night long; he'd jump on and off several times, as it suited him. Sometimes when I'd see Dodi the day after the dogs had slept in his room, he'd say, "God, Romeo didn't stop all night." But he really didn't mind. It was worth it to him to have the dogs with him.

Life with Dodi was very pleasant, right from the start. I particularly enjoyed the creativity involved in giving parties, although sometimes it could get hectic. On one particular occasion, about two or three months after I'd begun working for Dodi, he hosted a backyard barbecue, something that he always loved to do. As usual, many celebrities attended, including Tony Curtis, Ryan O'Neal, Paul Anka and Tina Sinatra. I had hired a chef, a waiter and a few other people I used to work with at Spago. We were going to serve grilled chicken breast, sausages, hamburgers and spareribs.

I asked Dodi, "Would you like a buffet? Or would you prefer that I go to each guest, tell him what we have, take his order and serve it?"

"Let's do a buffet," he replied.

I instructed the chef, waiters and busboys accordingly. We made our "game plan," aiming to get the buffet out and ready within thirty minutes, and everyone began to hustle. But just ten minutes before the buffet was completely laid out, Dodi came to me.

"Rene, you know what?" he said. This was my first experience with that particular phrase. I would learn later that it often meant a complete reversal of our plans.

"I think it would be better," he continued, "if you served each guest individually."

Great, I thought. We were just about ready to go.

"OK," I said, quickly rising to the occasion. "But it will take another forty minutes to move everything around and reset all the tables for regular service."

"No problem," Dodi said lightly. "Take your time."

We had been working quickly before, but now we really shifted into high gear, rushing the food back to the kitchen, taking away the buffet tables and setting up dining tables. Although we were moving as fast as we could, I could tell the guests were getting restless. Dodi asked me twice when we would be ready to serve.

Finally, Dodi appeared in the kitchen, asking me for the third time, "Rene, are we ready?"

Knowing that he was only concerned about his guests, not trying to give me a hard time, I drew myself up to my full height and said, with mock anger, "Sir, you handle the movies and let me handle the party."

"Yes, sir!" he replied, smiling, and left the kitchen. Soon after, we were ready to serve.

The party went smoothly, and everyone seemed to

enjoy the food, the atmosphere and the dancing. I knew Dodi, too, was pleased because at one point he grabbed me and wheeled me around the floor in a little dance. Yes, my new job was progressing well.

During the five years that I worked for Dodi in Beverly Hills, we lived in three different residences, each grander than the last. The first, on Beverly Drive just north of Santa Monica Boulevard, was in what they call "the flats." A one-story house, it was built in a "U" shape, wrapping around a large, beautiful garden. Most of the walls on the inside of the "U," facing the garden, were of glass, giving every room a perfect view of the garden. Our second house, located on Lexington Avenue north of Sunset, was a multilevel, open, modern place with a large entryway that led directly back to the dining area. In between the entryway and the dining area was a large, shallow reflecting pool complete with lily pads and floating candles. It was a very beautiful sight, especially in the evening when it was all lit up. The third house was the most exciting of all. It had a bowling alley, a disco, a private screening room and a spiral staircase leading up to the master bedroom, as well as a pool, Jacuzzi and tennis court. But we didn't spend all of our time in Beverly Hills. We also skied at two of the most popular resorts in the United States (Vail, Colorado, and Sun Valley, Idaho) and soaked up the sun in Cabo San Lucas, Mexico and other glamorous vacation spots.

Dodi was known for his thoughtfulness and generosity, not only for his high-profile celebrity friends. Whenever one of his employees had a birthday, he always made sure that there was a birthday cake, gathering everyone together to sing "Happy Birthday." He gave me time off for the Jewish holidays even though I was so nonobservant I didn't even know when they were! He often invited four or five people to join him on skiing vacations, paying to charter the jet that flew them there and to rent the chalet. And when they went out to eat, Dodi always paid. I went along on several trips myself and one time, when he was taking guests to a Moroccan restaurant, he insisted on my joining them because I was from Morocco and he knew I'd enjoy the food.

I recall yet another time when Dodi demonstrated his spontaneous generosity. While living in the house on Lexington, he was entertaining his good friend Christopher Lambert, the actor who played the leading role in *Greystoke: The Legend of Tarzan, Lord of the Apes*. When Christopher mentioned that he was going to St. Tropez on business, Dodi immediately offered him the use of his boat, the *Cujo*, which was docked there.

People often mistook his generosity for weakness, claiming that he didn't know how to say no, but they were wrong. To him, it was a pleasure to do something for others, to give a gift or help someone out. It wasn't something he felt trapped into doing. While it's true that he had difficulty saying no to friends or loved ones because of his naturally giving nature, he was nonetheless capable of it. I saw and heard him say it many times, sometimes with a fist on the table. And I saw him stick to those no's even when it was difficult. It's just that he preferred to say yes whenever possible.

Still, there were many who took advantage of him and I know this hurt him. Dodi usually came back from his dates looking relaxed and happy, but sometimes he'd return tense and irritated. Once, after an unhappy experience, he said to me, "Rene, can you believe women today?"

I brought him a cup of mint tea, which he liked to drink while winding down before bedtime, as he described his date with a woman who was obviously interested only in his money and what he could do for her. It was painful. Still, I knew that his no-strings-attached style of generosity would often attract that type of person. By that time I had been working for him for a couple of years, so I felt I could level with him.

"Mr. Fayed," I began, "I'm going to be honest with you. Everyone knows that you are a very generous man but, unfortunately, you are sometimes too generous too soon. Sometimes, even people who weren't after your money to begin with are swayed when you buy them expensive dinners, or invite them to one of your parties, or send them a present. Once they've had a taste of your money, they want more. You like to give people things, but it may get in the way of developing good relationships."

He listened carefully. After a moment he said, "So what do you think I should do?"

"I think you shouldn't be so giving, especially in the beginning. You have a lot of qualities that could make a woman fall in love with you. See if she falls in love with who you are inside. If she does, great. Then you can spend money on her."

A hush fell between us. I don't think too many people had ever spoken to him that way.

He gave me a measured look and replied, "I think you're right."

I continued to work happily for Dodi Fayed, finding it easy to accommodate his wishes and fit into his schedule. Approximately every two months he would take a trip to Europe for a week or two to attend to family business in London or Paris, and I would be off work (although still on the payroll) until he returned. I truly had the ideal job.

Then, in June of 1994, Dodi called me. "Rene, I have to spend some time in Europe," he said. "I'd like it very much if you would come with me."

I was torn. My young son, Bruno, lived in Los Angeles, and moving to Europe would mean leaving my family and friends. On the other hand, my enviable job—working for an easygoing man who led an exciting lifestyle and treated me wonderfully—would go up in smoke if I didn't follow him.

"It will only be for six months to a year," Dodi promised. "Then we'll come back to L.A."

Well, that didn't sound so bad. Six months could go by in the blink of an eye. Besides, by sheer coincidence, my other son, Alain, was moving to Paris at the time, and I also had several friends there. It might not be so bad for a little while. I decided then and there to move to Europe with Dodi. Obviously, I really wanted to keep my job, certain that there was no other like it. Dodi was very pleased.

My first assignment was to get the dogs, Romeo and Shoe, from Beverly Hills to the Fayed family home in Gstaad, Switzerland. Like the other chalets, Chalet Tannegg, as it was called, was a grand wooden building with a slanted roof. Flowers and other designs were carved into the wood. There was a yard in front, perhaps fifty yards wide and thirty yards deep, with trees all around the periphery for privacy. My room was on the lower level, and we fixed up a room near mine for Romeo and Shoe. The ground floor contained bedrooms, a living room, a kitchen and an office with a small library. The upstairs, where the decor was warmer and more elaborate, was set aside for Mr. Al Fayed.

I waited there for three months while Dodi decided whether we would live in London, Paris or there in Switzerland. Once he had decided on Paris, I was installed in Dodi's beautiful apartment on rue Arsene-Houssaye, where my quarters consisted of a small living room and bedroom next to the kitchen.

My workload was relatively light. Dodi spent much of his time in London, as he was on the boards of both Harrods and Turnbull & Asser. On the infrequent occasions that he was in Paris, he threw very few parties. Guests were usually taken out to dinner at his father's fabled Hotel Ritz, which was only a ten-minute drive from the apartment, or to some fine restaurant. As a result, I was no longer an entertainment director or personal assistant. I was now a full-fledged butler, which meant that I served cocktails and meals to Dodi and his guests, sometimes prepared simple dinners, ordered food from the Ritz and made sure everything in the apartment was in order.

I also looked after the dogs and walked them daily. The Paris apartment was not an ideal location for them because there was nowhere they could run free. So, following Dodi's suggestion, I took them to the beautiful, far-reaching grounds at Windsor Villa, the gorgeous former home of the Duke and Duchess of Windsor, now owned by the Fayed family. There, the dogs were able to run to their hearts' content on grassy lawns, and from that point on I would take them there almost every day.

Although it was not the social whirl that we'd enjoyed in Beverly Hills, life with Dodi was still good. Little was expected of me while he was away, and when he returned he was always very easy to please. And I knew that this living situation was only temporary; Dodi himself had told me it would be only six months to a year at the most. I was certain that any day he would come to me and say, "Rene, pack your bags! We're moving back to L.A.!" But as it turned out, Dodi's business obligations required him to stay in Paris for more than three years. Although I missed my home, I enjoyed working for him so much that I decided to stay. I knew we'd go back to L.A. eventually. In the meantime, I would have to learn to be patient.

CHAPTER

3

The Romance Begins

B*rrrring, brrrring!* The ringing of the phone split the silence that surrounded me as I sat reading in my quarters on that warm July evening in 1997. We had been living in Paris for more than three years, and I was almost used to the sleepy pace that life had taken on. By this time I had accepted the fact that a return to L.A. was still in the not-so-near future. At the moment, Dodi was vacationing with his family on their yacht in the south of France, so I'd had time to become absorbed in the newspaper I was reading. But I'd learned that one of the conditions of my job was to be ready for anything at a moment's notice, so I quickly picked up the receiver.

"Hello?"

"Hello, Rene," countered the brisk voice of Dodi's secretary in London. "This is Sinead. Just letting you know that Mr. Fayed will arrive tomorrow and you should have everything ready."

"Of course," I replied. "Absolutely. I'll make sure everything is perfect, as usual."

My boss was always very considerate—he never just showed up after he'd been away, but either called himself or had someone else call to give me advance warning. I appreciated this quality; because he respected my privacy, I could relax more completely while he was away. But now my relaxing was over and it was time to go to work.

"Making sure everything was perfect" was a pretty good description of what I'd been doing for the past three years, ever since I became a butler. It meant calling the Ritz to order Dodi's favorite foods (smoked salmon, crab salad, salade Niçoise, fruit, cheese and much more), his favorite drinks (Baron de'L, 1994, a dry, rich and fruity white, and a little bit of Stolichnaya vodka) and fresh flowers for the arrangements that we changed twice a week. He had a fondness for aromatic candles, especially those that smelled like lilac, so I made sure we had plenty of those as well. I also routinely checked to see that everything was clean and in order in the house; if not, I'd take the matter up with the housekeeper.

The door to our building was located on rue Arsene-Houssaye, but the apartment was so large that its windows actually faced three streets, one of which was the celebrated Avenue des Champs-Elysées. A narrow balcony with a wrought-iron fence jutted out from the base of these windows, making it an ideal place to watch the annual Bastille Day parade. Unfortunately, you were quite conspicuous to the crowd below, so my boss rarely went out on the balcony for more than a minute or two.

We were situated in an extremely high rent district, about a block from L'Etoile and directly across the street from the famous "Drug Store," a modern glassed-in building boasting shops, restaurants, boutiques and the pharmacy for which it was named. There was hardly a better view in all of Paris. And despite the fact that we were right on the busy and noisy Champs, it was very quiet in the apartment. Double panes of glass kept the noise out.

The ten-room apartment, which sprawled over the entire second floor of the building, was old and very elegant, with the lavish, delicate, neoclassic style of Louis XVI evident in the walls and draperies. An ornate Louis XVI-style gilded chandelier dominated the entryway, spilling its light over an intricately patterned pink, black and white marble floor. The apartment boasted floor-to-ceiling windows, ornately carved moldings, brocade furnishings and gilded trim, with wealth evident everywhere. But scattered among the antiques were some signs that a younger, hipper person was living there.

In the main living room, with its two overstuffed modern sofas, pink marble-topped coffee table and white marble mantlepiece, a large TV set stared blankly from the corner of the room. Framed pictures of Dodi's father and other family members, as well as many modern-day movie stars, such as Daryl Hannah, Burt Reynolds, Tony Curtis, Christopher Lambert, Gene Kelly and Timothy Dalton, all posing affably with my boss, were all around. And stuffed animals seemed to pop up everywhere, especially in Dodi's bedroom, where three stuffed bears from Harrods sat on a table next to the marble fireplace. He had even put three large bears on chairs in the dining room, as if they were invited guests waiting to be served. Also in Dodi's bedroom was a display of model airplanes, proof that the lively, fun-loving child inside him was still very much alive.

I wandered through marble bathrooms and exquisite guest rooms, past priceless tapestries and over Persian carpets. I opened the mirrored wardrobe doors and saw that everything was still neatly arranged, as it was when he left. His fifteen dark Armani suits hung mutely, his four pairs of cowboy boots stood side by side at attention, while his jackets and shirts waited patiently to be chosen for the next evening out. The underwear, socks, shorts and sweatpants lay neatly folded in their labeled drawers. All was in readiness.

The next day, with cupboards stocked, flowers fresh and beautifully arranged in their vases and the entire apartment gleaming like a highly polished gem, I, too, was ready. When the call came, I answered the phone confidently.

"Hello, Rene!" The warm, friendly voice of my boss crackled across the line. "I'm at the hotel." I knew, of course, that he meant the Hotel Ritz, that distinguished 142-room architectural landmark that graced the famed Place Vendôme. Like other members of the Fayed family, Dodi had a luxurious suite at the hotel, although he usually stayed at the apartment when in Paris.

"Did you have a nice holiday, sir?" I asked, wishing I had just spent a week on the Cote d'Azur, the famous "Blue Coast" in the south of France.

"Excellent, Rene. Just excellent," he said enthusiastically. His tone quickly changed as his voice became very serious. "Listen, Rene. You must bring me some clothes for tonight. I'm going to have dinner with Princess Diana!"

"Diana!" I exclaimed. There was hardly a more famous woman in the entire world—her picture was in the paper almost every day. I knew they had met before, and that Dodi had joined the Fayed family vacation with the princess and her two boys in St. Tropez the past few days. But I was surprised to hear that they were going on a date.

"Yes," he said, "so please bring me some clothes, a tie and some shoes." He sounded happier and more animated than I'd ever heard him before.

"Oh, and Rene," he added. "Please. I want this to be discreet, so dress casually when you come here. Don't wear anything to draw attention to yourself. Philippe will leave now to pick you up."

Philippe Dourneau was Dodi's regular chauffeur in Paris, so I knew him well. I had always liked Philippe. He was very energetic, friendly, totally devoted to Dodi and always very professional. So I was not surprised when Philippe, with his customary punctuality, rapped on the apartment door within twenty minutes of my boss' phone call.

Dodi hadn't specified which clothes he wanted me to bring. Just to be safe I brought two suits, a couple of dress shirts, three ties and two pairs of shoes so that he would have a choice. Philippe helped me load these clothes into the big black Mercedes 600; then we hopped in and cruised down the Champs toward the Ritz. We were both very excited about the fact that Dodi was going out with Diana and chatted about it during the ride.

The Hotel Ritz is an awe-inspiring edifice built in 1898 and purchased in 1979 by my boss' father for about thirty million dollars. He then spent at least one hundred fifty million renovating, modernizing and restoring it to its original splendor. No matter how many times I visited the hotel, I found myself awestruck by its beauty and opulence.

On this particular visit, Philippe and I parked in back of the hotel to avoid attention. There, we were greeted by Claude Roulet, assistant to the hotel's president. If I hadn't realized it before, I'd certainly know by his presence that our little errand was of great importance. Mr. Roulet personally escorted me to Dodi's suite and knocked on the door.

The Dodi who opened the door looked happier and more excited than he had at any time during the seven years I'd worked for him. I'd last seen him only ten days before, but the difference in his demeanor was dramatic. Although he usually seemed cheerful and serene, with a friendly smile, he now seemed to be, as we say in French, *joyeux*, or "joyful." Clearly this was an important and happy occasion.

I went immediately to the closet, hung up his clothes, put his shoes in their proper place and then turned to him, awaiting further orders.

"Have you seen my suite here at the hotel before, Rene?" Dodi asked.

I hadn't, so he graciously gave me a quick tour. Then his mood turned serious.

"Rene," he instructed, "I want you to go with Philippe to Lucas Carton, the restaurant where the princess and I will be dining tonight. Find out where the table is that they've reserved for us. I've asked for something private, so go there and double check."

"As you wish, Mr. Fayed," I replied.

"And don't tell them who I'm coming with," he added a bit anxiously. "I don't want to draw attention to us. Just say it's a special guest."

A special guest, indeed, I thought. None other than the most famous, most photographed woman in the world!

Ah, but there was one problem, so just before I reached the door I turned back to my boss.

"Uh, Mr. Fayed," I asked hesitantly, "when I meet the princess, what shall I call her?"

He stopped for a moment, stumped.

"I don't know," he finally said, with a small shrug and a smile. I would have to figure it out myself later.

As I went downstairs to the lobby, I felt strangely giddy, almost as if I myself were going on a date with the glamorous woman. I had, of course, met and served many of Dodi's women friends, all of whom were beautiful and some of whom were quite famous. But this one was really special—truly in a class by herself. I wondered what she would be like.

Philippe and I took off on our errand, but we had

gone only a few blocks when he looked in the rearview mirror and frowned.

"What's wrong?" I asked, noticing his expression.

"Hmmm," he mused. "I think we're being followed."

Looking into the mirror but not turning around, I asked, "Which car?"

"The mini Cooper," he said, referring to a tiny car that the paparazzi often use because it's fast, maneuverable and excellent for following cars through crowded city streets.

"But why us?" I asked innocently. " We're nobody."

"I guess *he* thinks we're somebody," replied Philippe. "I'll drive around for a few minutes going nowhere, to see if he's following us."

We found a circular intersection and drove completely around it five times. The mini Cooper stayed behind us all the way.

"What are we going to do?" I asked Philippe, getting a little worried. "We can't go to the restaurant with him following us. If he finds out where we're going, he'll call the others and the place will be a zoo."

"Don't worry," Philippe calmly replied. "I'll lose him." Thanks to Philippe's expert maneuvering, by the time we reached Lucas Carton, the photographer was nowhere in sight. He dropped me off and drove down the street to park. He didn't want anyone to see the Fayed car, one that many people recognized, sitting in front of the restaurant and call out the paparazzi.

Meanwhile, inside the restaurant I located the maitre d' and politely inquired as to where Mr. Fayed and his special guest would be seated that evening. I impressed upon him that privacy was very much desired. Since the restaurant had been notified only a few hours in advance, the maitre d' had had to hastily rearrange the evening's seating in order to place Dodi and his special guest in an alcove. It was not absolutely, completely private, but it would do.

Mission accomplished, I returned to the lobby of the Ritz and sat in a corner chair facing the elevator. I didn't have to wait long—soon, the elevator doors opened and there was Dodi with one of the most beautiful women I had ever seen—very tall, blond and radiating a glowing energy that I could almost feel. I was surprised to see that she looked even more spectacular in person than in photographs. Casually but elegantly dressed in light blue pants, a white shirt and a beautiful navy blue blazer, she was so magnetic it was impossible to look away from her.

The first glimpse I got of the two of them told me volumes. They were standing close together, shoulders just barely touching, and although they both faced forward, their heads were inclined toward each other as they exchanged a few words. She said something to him in a low voice, their eyes locked and they shared an intimate laugh. It was as if they were in on some amusing secret that no one else was privileged to know. In that first second, I could tell that something special was going on between them. I was absolutely thrilled for both of them.

I did not rush up to my boss, but instead stood up so that he could see me and waited to be approached. One of the most important parts of my job was to be invisible when the situation warranted it, so I simply waited for some sign. After speaking briefly with the concierge, Dodi approached me and quietly asked, "Rene, how was the restaurant?"

"Mr. Fayed," I said, matching his quiet tone, "you are going to be pleased. They've changed the entire layout of the tables to give you some privacy."

"Did you tell them who is coming with me?" he inquired a bit worriedly.

"No, sir. Just that it is someone special, so they should give you their very best service."

He nodded gravely. "Good. It seems that if anyone finds out, then the paparazzi know, and they ruin everything. You did a good job. We're going to have dinner, perhaps take a walk, then come to the apartment. I'll see you there later."

"Very good, sir," I replied. And with that they were off.

As soon as I returned to the apartment, I called my eighty-year-old uncle Jacques, a well-educated man who has been everywhere and done everything. If anyone would know what I should call the princess, he would.

"Call her Madame," he told me. And so I did.

Later that night, shortly after midnight, as planned, Dodi brought Diana back to the apartment, where I stood ready with champagne, aperitifs, coffee and just about anything else they could have wanted. When they buzzed at the front door downstairs, I could see it was Dodi, but, as I had always done, I answered the intercom with "Hello?"

This time he laughed, knowing that I could see full well who it was.

"Rene, don't you recognize me?" he retorted. I could tell he was in a very good mood.

"Of course, sir," I said, immediately buzzing them in.

I was very excited and more than a little nervous as I waited by the open door for my boss and the princess to get off the elevator. As Dodi ushered the princess in, I found myself in awe of the woman I'd seen so many times in magazines and newspapers. She was much more beautiful in person, as I've said earlier, but she also had some kind of aura around her—a mixture of warmth, friendliness, compassion and a sense of fun. She was truly magnetic.

"Hello," she said cheerily, looking me right in the eye with a steady, friendly gaze. "I'm Diana."

"I'm Rene," I replied. "It is a pleasure to meet you, Madame."

We both nodded our heads, but did not shake hands, and that was almost a good thing because my palms had begun to sweat. Although in the course of my career I had served many important people, from movie stars to royalty, I had rarely been this nervous. Not just because she was *the* Princess Diana, but because I knew that she was very important to my boss. More than ever before, I wanted things to go perfectly that night.

After handing me his jacket, Dodi escorted Diana into the living room, where he immediately took her to the window to show her our incredible view of the Champs-Elysées. On that beautiful, clear night, the dazzling lights seemed to offer themselves up like an exhibition of the crown jewels. The princess appeared impressed and said all of the right things ("Oh, it's just lovely, what a beautiful view"), but very quickly turned her gaze back to Dodi. To me, it was obvious that on that night she was much more interested in her companion than she was in views—even outstanding ones. Certainly the same could be said for him, as they gazed at each other and moved toward the couch. One of the very first things I noticed about the two of them as a couple was the amount of eye contact they made—it seemed as if they almost never looked away. And I could sense that they were very comfortable together; the first-date "jitters" were nowhere in sight.

They settled themselves on the comfortable, over-stuffed couch, sitting close to each other but angled inward so they could continue to look into each other's eyes. Asking only for Evian water and some Julio Iglesias music, they began to talk, easily, and without the self-consciousness, defensiveness or posturing so common on first dates. They seemed to be kindred spirits, delighted at finding each other. Something special was definitely in the air.

Once they seemed comfortable and satisfied, I retreated to my quarters, returning every ten minutes or so to see if they needed anything. This was a rather delicate task—I wanted to be available so that my boss wouldn't have to come looking for me, but I certainly didn't want to interrupt or embarrass them. So I would very discreetly look in and catch my boss' eye. They sat side by side on the couch, holding hands as they listened to the music, and each time, Dodi waved his hand slightly to signify that I was not needed.

In between my forays to the living room, I watched television as I kept an eye on Romeo and Shoe. About midway through the princess' visit, Romeo suddenly pricked up his ears and began to growl. Before I could grab him, he raced out of my quarters and straight into the long hallway toward the entryway. I heard a scream. Rushing after him, I saw that Romeo, all seventy-five pounds of him, had playfully leaped on Diana and knocked her off balance! He wanted some fun and games. Evidently Dodi had been giving the princess a tour of the apartment and when he opened the door to the hallway, Romeo heard it and decided to investigate.

Mortified, I immediately tried to coax Romeo back to me so I could grab his collar and take him back to my quarters.

"Come on, baby. Come on, baby..." I pleaded.

The princess smiled and said wryly, "You call *that* a baby?" Then she laughed good-naturedly, easing my embarrassment and letting me know it was no big deal. And after that, she always seemed to have a special fondness for Romeo.

Later, after Dodi had taken Diana to her suite at the Ritz, he asked me in that man-to-man way, "So, Rene, what do you think of the princess?"

"I think she is gorgeous," I replied truthfully, "and very, very nice."

He nodded, his eyes taking on a soft glow.

"She also has a good sense of humor, even when dogs are jumping on her," he said, looking at me slyly. Then he laughed.

I was relieved that he wasn't angry about the Romeo escapade. Instead, he seemed happy and excited. I was excited too, hoping that something would spark and a relationship would be built. My boss was a man who had an abundance of material things, but I knew he was lonely. He hadn't yet found his special someone, a soul mate, and this gave his life a certain emptiness, I felt. All the money, cars, homes, yachts and beautiful women in the world couldn't seem to fill the void in his heart. He needed to find true love. Perhaps Diana would be the one to make his life complete. With all my heart I hoped it would be so.

Often, when Dodi was feeling very content, he would ask for mint tea and a cigar, and that's exactly what he requested at that moment. He returned to the living room, where he puffed on his cigar, lost in thought. He didn't even glance out the window—he just sat staring into space, perhaps dreaming of the glorious possibilities his future might hold.

Although their romance was brand new, Dodi Fayed and Princess Diana had actually met more than ten years earlier when the Harrods polo team played Prince Charles' team at Windsor. Their paths had crossed a few more times over the years, but they remained acquaintances only. However, the princess did develop a friendship with Dodi's father, who had been a friend of her own father, and she often visited him at his office when she shopped at Harrods, her favorite department store.

After her separation from the Prince of Wales, Mr. Al Fayed repeatedly invited Diana and her sons to join him and his family at their various vacation homes, to no avail. Then, in early June 1997, the two of them were seated together at a benefit dinner for the English National Ballet. The princess asked Mr. Fayed where he planned to vacation with his family that summer, to which he replied, "St. Tropez. Would you like to come with us?" This time, the princess accepted.

So on Friday, July 11, a Harrods helicopter winged its way to Kensington Palace, picked up Diana and her two sons, William and Harry, and flew them to Barrow Green Court, the Al Fayed mansion at Oxted, in the beautiful English countryside.

Barrow Green Court (or Oxted, as we always called it) is a splendid Elizabethan manor with beautifully manicured lawns and gardens that rival those at royal residences around the world. It was here that the princess and her boys had a light lunch with Mr. Al Fayed, his wife, Heini, and their four children, before departing for the nearby airport at Stansted. After a two-and-a-half hour flight on the Fayeds' private jet, they arrived in Nice and were driven to a small harbor at St. Laurent-du-Var. They were finally able to board the magnificent motor yacht, the *Jonikal*.

The last word in sailing luxury, this 180-foot boat has several levels, many sleeping cabins, three exquisitely appointed living rooms, an outdoor covered lounge, two kitchens and a crew of sixteen. It is truly a floating palace.

Once its small party of vacationers was aboard, the *Jonikal* took off for the Fayed villa, Castel Ste. Helene, a fabulous ten-acre estate on the cliffs overlooking St. Tropez.

There, the princess and her sons were assured their privacy as long as they stayed within the confines of the villa. They had their own swimming pool, tanning deck, gardens, butler and cook. Unfortunately, if they ventured down to the villa's private beach to go Jet-Skiing, sailing or scuba diving, they became prime targets for the paparazzi. And the stalking began right at the start of their holiday, continuing to plague them through the last day.

At one point, Diana was annoyed enough to take matters into her own hands. Spying a group of six journalists in a motorboat about one hundred fifty yards offshore, she and a bodyguard hopped into a launch and made a beeline for them. They pulled up next to the paparazzi boat and the princess asked them point-blank how long they were planning on maintaining their vigil. The attention, she told them, was embarrassing and she was afraid her sons' holiday was going to be ruined. She also hinted that she might leave Britain one day because the endless scrutiny was so hard to bear. The journalists agreed that they would leave her and the boys alone at night when they went into town—as long as they got some good shots during the day.

Mr. Al Fayed was upset at the discomfort the press was causing his famous guest. Eager to provide maximum enjoyment for her holiday, he thought she would have more fun with a companion nearer her own age. It was July 14, Bastille Day, and there would be a beautiful fireworks display in Cannes that night. Mr. Al Fayed called his son and asked him to join them for the evening's festivities.

I was with Dodi at the apartment when he got the call. That morning, he had watched the Bastille Day parade on the Champs-Elysées from the apartment window and was looking forward to a quiet day at home. As soon as he spoke to his father, however, he was galvanized into action.

It was during those few days aboard the *Jonikal* and at Castel Ste. Helene, against a backdrop of warm summer sun and the dazzling blue Mediterranean Sea, that Dodi and Diana began to develop feelings for each other. They were together for at least a few hours every day for five days, before the princess and her sons had to return to London. Then, just six days later, he called me from the Ritz, excitedly telling me that he and Diana were to have their first date that night.

The princess returned to London the day after their Parisian dinner date, and Dodi followed a couple of days later for business purposes. Then, just three days after he left, he called me from London.

"Stand by for the next few days," Dodi told me urgently. "I'll need you to make preparations." He went on joyfully, "The princess and I are going to take a little trip on the *Jonikal*—this time alone!"

Evidently, the dinner date had gone very well.

CHAPTER

4

On the Jonikal

Four days later, just as he had promised, Dodi and the princess were ready to take another Mediterranean cruise. This time, though, there would be far fewer people accompanying them: Captain Luigi and a small Italian crew to do the actual sailing; John, the bodyguard; two young women, Debbie and Mary, who set the tables, cleaned and did laundry (Debbie also helped me serve, and she took care of the princess' personal needs); Christiano, an outstanding chef; and, of course, myself. Considering the two principals involved, this was truly a skeleton crew, and about as "alone" as they could possibly be. (There might have been even more people, for Diana was entitled to royal bodyguards at all times. I guessed that she gave up that right in exchange for greater privacy.)

I flew from Paris to Nice, that tourist mecca in the south of France, where I was picked up by taxi and taken to the little harbor of St. Laurent-du-Var. Then a small boat took me out to the awe-inspiring *Jonikal*. Since it had been only recently purchased by Mr. Al Fayed, I had never seen it before, and an impressive sight it was. My God! I had worked in palatial residences in Beverly Hills, I lived in the sumptuous Fayed apartment in Paris, I had been to the Fayed home in Gstaad and scores of other impressive places, but I had never seen anything like this! It was absolutely unmatched for majesty and beauty.

One hundred eighty feet long with twelve sleeping cabins and (usually) a crew of sixteen, the *Jonikal* was truly a vessel worthy of royalty. In addition to the various working areas below (engine room, galley, crew quarters, etc.), it had two levels plus a sundeck on top, three living rooms, a dining room, an outdoor lounge area, two kitchens and even its own helipad. As I toured the yacht for the first time, I was awestruck by the luxurious appointments—varnished timberwork, gleaming parquet floors, Persian carpets, soft-as-a-cloud overstuffed couches and fine art—all of which combined to create an atmosphere of warmth, elegance and comfort.

My favorite place was the main living room, with its many intimate sitting areas sporting pale yellow, royal blue and white couches and easy chairs with highly polished hardwood coffee tables. The walls were decorated with intricately carved, thickly varnished wainscoting on the lower half and a fine, pale yellow fabric above—the perfect backdrop for the fine art that adorned them. The ceiling was a combination of varnished timberwork and mirrored glass that gave the room an open but warm feeling.

This room led to an open-air salon at the back of the boat. There, a very long blue and brown patterned semicircular couch ran along the perimeter, with a couple of bolted-down round tables set in front of it. Movable upholstered chairs and stools were arranged around the tables. I could see that this would be a comfortable place to sit and have cocktails while watching the sun set—informal, comfortable, open to the air and yet covered. On the other side of the main living room, toward the front of the vessel, were two smaller living rooms. Beyond a staircase lay Dodi's massive master suite, which was flanked by two guest suites, and running all the way around the periphery of the yacht was a wide, wooden walkway. You could get plenty of exercise by jogging completely around the *Jonikal* once or twice.

I don't know nautical terms, so I simply called this main deck the first level, ignoring the crew, engine and other areas below. Above was the second level, which had, from front to back, the pilot house, the captain's quarters, my room and the small kitchen where I often stationed myself, the security room where John stayed, plus some cozy sitting/dining areas. Behind that, through sliding doors, was the main dining table and beyond that, at the very back of the boat, was a storage area for the two smaller boats and the Jet Skis. Perched above all this, on the very top level, was the sundeck and helipad.

After being shown around and meeting everyone, I was taken to my cabin. Although most of the crew shared the small rooms down below next to the galley, I had a cabin all to myself. It was located on the second level, right next to the captain's quarters, and in truth, the word "cabin" was a completely inadequate description. This gorgeous, wood-paneled (I believe it was teak) room was outfitted to sleep three, with a bunk bed plus a single, and its own beautifully appointed marble bathroom. Rectangular, curtained windows looked out over the sea, and the room's position on the second level, far away from the noisy galley and crew quarters, ensured that I would have plenty of peace and quiet.

As I set down my luggage and looked around, the first words I uttered were, "My God, I could live here!" But I had no time to waste; Dodi and the princess were expected soon. Lolling about in my splendid "cabin," fantasizing about being rich and famous, would have to wait.

My first task was to familiarize myself with that massive yacht. It was imperative that I knew where everything was, how to get from here to there, how the music system worked and so on, before they arrived. I didn't want to be caught short, having to answer a request with, "Of course. But please tell me where I can find that?" I knew Dodi would understand if I had not mastered everything, since this was my first time on the yacht. But I myself wanted to be well informed and on top of things.

Decending to the lower level, I first paid a visit to the boat's galley to meet the chef, Christiano. He was busily working his magic in the most elaborate kitchen I'd ever seen afloat. Unlike the tiny galleys found on most boats, this one sported a walk-in refrigerator and a walk-in

Princess Diana looking glamorous during a visit to the Tate Gallery a few months before the beginning of her romance with Dodi. (Rex Features)

The lavish apartment building on rue Arsene-Houssaye in Paris, where I first served Princess Diana and where, much later, I heard the terrible news of the accident. (Rex Features)

The grand foyer of the Paris apartment, where I first met Diana—and where I said farewell on that final, fateful night. (*Sunday Mirror*)

The living room in Paris (above) where the couple enjoyed music and quiet moments together. It was on the coffee table that I found the wine glass—the last item Diana touched before leaving on that final night. Adjacent to the living room is the dining room (below), where Dodi sat a Harrods bear as a permanent guest. (*Sunday Mirror*)

Ornate gilt carvings and framed photos fill the mantelpiece in the side salon (above) of the Paris apartment. Dodi's majestic bedroom (below) was fit for a king. (*Sunday Mirror*)

The sumptuous bathroom off Dodi's bedroom, complete with Jacuzzi. (*Sunday Mirror*)

Dodi's beloved dog, Romeo, pictured in a photo in his Paris bedroom. (*Sunday Mirror*)

Dodi's study (above) at the Park Lane apartment in London, where the couple dined while holding their plates on their laps. The bedroom (below) reflected Dodi's modern taste in furnishings. (*Sunday Mirror*)

The Fayed mansion at Oxted, where the lovers found a haven from the paparazzi. (*Sunday Mirror*)

The Princess looking tranquil and happy in Bosnia just after her first cruise alone with Dodi. (Popperfoto)

The lavish interior of the Gulfstream IV jet. Here I am waiting for the lovers to board for our return to Paris after our second, final, cruise.

One of the many paparazzi boats that plagued us on our second cruise.

freezer big enough to store a major feast. The pantry that adjoined it, with its loads of canned and boxed foods, resembled a small but well-stocked grocery store. Of one thing I could be sure—we certainly wouldn't want for food on this trip!

"So, Christiano," I said, "I know that Mr. Fayed will want to know what we've got for dinner. What shall I tell him?"

Christiano was well prepared. He had smoked salmon canapés for appetizers, followed by a seafood salad with a choice of three vinaigrettes. For the main course, Christiano suggested sea bass grilled with vegetables, and for dessert sorbet or chocolate mousse.

"Sounds good to me." I said, and went back to the second level to await the arrival of my boss and his princess. Then, seemingly out of nowhere, the Fayed family jet, a Gulfstream IV, appeared in the sky and began its descent into the Nice airport. This galvanized everybody into last-minute preparations. Debbie and Mary scurried around arranging pillows, polishing brass and making sure every room was in perfect order. The cook shifted into high gear, whipping together hors d'oeuvres, fresh salad dressing and chopped vegetables. Captain Luigi and the security guard hopped into the tender and headed for shore while I changed into my butler's, or "night," uniform. (This is what I wore at all times while on duty at the apartment, but on the boat I'd wear shorts and T-shirts during the day.) When Dodi and Diana finally arrived, all of us aboard the *Jonikal* were as ready as we could possibly be.

Diana was radiant, blue eyes sparkling, matching her beautiful powder blue jacket and pants. Shoes in hand, she was barefoot, and had brought only one bag, laughingly commenting that she liked to travel light. As before, I found her extremely charming and vivacious, smiling and greeting everyone as she came aboard. Whenever she was introduced to someone, no matter what their station in life, she would look them in the eye, smile warmly and without hesitation extend her hand to deliver a warm handshake. "Hello! I'm Diana," she'd say cheerily, something I found refreshingly unpretentious.

As soon as she saw me, the princess stuck out her hand and said, smiling, "Hello, Rene! It's very nice to see you again."

"Madame," I replied, delighted to be recognized by her, "the pleasure is mine."

As time went by, I noticed that she made it a point to know (and use) the names of everyone on the yacht. She asked for very little, and when she did, it was always with the utmost politeness, never failing to say "Please" and "Thank you." Strange as it may sound, she managed to make everyone around her feel like an equal. I knew we were all in for an enjoyable trip.

Dodi was to stay in the master cabin, with the princess in the one next to it. I could tell that both were excited and happy to be aboard as he escorted her to her room.

"It's just so wonderful to be back," I heard her say to him as they walked down the hallway, arm in arm. He smiled and said tenderly, while looking right into her eyes, "It's wonderful to have *you* back." Their eyes held for a moment, then she squeezed his arm a little tighter and laid her head on his shoulder, just for a second, as if to say "Thank you."

He left her at the door of her room to freshen up, but before heading for his own quarters, Dodi pulled me aside to ask about dinner. I was able to recite Christiano's menu without hesitation and Dodi was pleased.

"That sounds fine," he said. "Serve the appetizers and our dinner on the first level, in the open-air salon. Oh, and Rene, let's have some nuts and a little beluga caviar. She loves caviar."

The open-air salon at the back of the boat sported a long, curved couch that ran along the perimeter of the back area, two low tables (perhaps eighteen inches high) and some cozy upholstered chairs. It made a lovely, casual setting. That first evening, after I had covered the tables with fine linen, set out vases of fresh flowers (we purchased new bouquets whenever we went into port), lit several candles and made sure the table looked exquisite, I stood by, waiting for Dodi and the princess to arrive. Moments later, they came to the table, holding hands and laughing. It was clear they were very happy to be reunited, and just the way their shoulders brushed together suggested that some sort of bond had already formed. They were both wearing T-shirts, she in shorts and he in long pants—and that was the casual way they would dress for the entire cruise. They definitely didn't want it to be a fancy, dress-up affair; they wanted to relax.

As I pulled out a chair for the princess and seated her, she exclaimed, "Oh, caviar, my favorite."

"Madame," I ventured, "we have plenty of caviar for you. Would you like anything else?"

She smiled up at me. "A glass of wine, please, Rene."

"Of course. Is Baron de'L OK with you?" This was Dodi's favorite wine.

"Yes, thank you," she replied.

I knew that she drank only a little, enough for taste and enjoyment, and didn't want more than a half glass at a time. I poured each of them a half glass of Baron de'L.

After watching for a few minutes to make sure they had everything they needed, I quietly withdrew. The sea was sapphire blue and very calm as they watched a red-orange sun melt slowly into the horizon—as perfect an evening as nature had ever created. Each time I returned to see if they wanted anything, I found them chatting away, often laughing, heads together. Sometimes she touched his arm when she spoke. They had pulled their chairs closer together, as if being even a few inches apart was too much. The electricity between them could have lit up the night.

Thus began their first stay alone on the *Jonikal*—quietly, pleasantly, peacefully. Who could ever have foreseen just how precious and few these golden moments would be?

My daily routine was quite simple. My sole duty was to take care of Dodi and Diana, so for me the trip was almost a vacation. Captain Luigi was, of course, responsible for the navigation and anything to do with the boat. Debbie and Mary had to arise at seven to set breakfast tables for Dodi and Diana, as well as the crew below. They also did the laundry and made up the rooms. In addition, Debbie assisted me in serving and would take care of any of the princess' personal needs. I, on the other hand, could sleep until nine and still have plenty of time to get ready. (Since I stayed up until Dodi and Diana went to bed, usually after one, and because Dodi had told me that he would never need me before ten-thirty in the morning, I could sleep late.) I'd shower, shave, put on some shorts and a shirt and be on deck before ten.

I would then double-check to make sure that everything was ready. Breakfast was always served at the large oval dining table on the second deck. There would be a mouth-watering array of at least ten different kinds of sliced fresh fruit, a dozen just-baked croissants, three or four kinds of jam and Evian water. Then, of course, they could order anything else they wanted—freshly blended carrot juice, orange juice, omelets, salmon toast, eggs Benedict or whatever. The porcelain china and solid silverware was always perfectly arranged, and there were fresh flowers in a vase on the table. On that first morning, satisfied that all was in order, I stood by, soaking up the wonderfully warm Mediterranean sun, looking out over the deep blue water toward the beautiful coastline of Monaco.

The princess was the first to arrive at the table that morning. Wearing a very attractive pastel aqua one-piece swimsuit, she was slim and tall, with an absolutely beautiful body. She could easily have gotten away with wearing a bikini, but during the entire trip she wore only one-piece suits. She had a new one every day, each in a beautiful pastel color—yellow, green, blue and soft white. The only exception was a wild animal print. My guess is that she probably wore one-piece suits because there were several men on the yacht and she always wanted to be properly covered and modest. But it also may have been a gesture of respect to Dodi; in no way did she ever flaunt herself. Yet she was always very pleasant to look at, with her smiling face, beautiful blond hair and graceful figure.

Each morning she would greet me cheerily with, "Rene, how are you? How was your night?"

"It was excellent, Madame, thank you very much," I'd reply, as I pulled out her chair and seated her. This same ritual would be repeated every morning of the trip, with the princess always asking about my health and the quality of my sleep.

Soon, Dodi would join her and they'd begin what was to become their morning routine. First, they would greet each other with a hug and a kiss, chatting a little about how well each had slept, what the weather was like, and so forth. They laughed a little and the conversation flowed easily; they would often hold hands. Sometimes she'd prop her elbow on the table and rest her hand on Dodi's shoulder—a sweet, affectionate gesture, I thought. Then they'd settle down to read the newspapers (the London *Times, Daily Mail* or whatever else was available). They liked to read certain sections of the paper to each other, especially things they found to be funny, and as they read, I'd bring their coffee and, a bit later, their breakfast. The princess always started with a double espresso plus a little milk, but no sugar. Dodi took his espresso black. The princess would then eat a small amount of fruit, while Dodi usually asked for scrambled eggs (whites only, no yolks).

At this leisurely pace, breakfast usually lasted at least an hour and a half. Eventually, the two would saunter up to the sundeck, with its wonderfully comfortable yellow-cushioned lounge chairs. For the next hour or two they would settle down for some serious suntanning while tackling their business chores. If they asked, I would pipe in soft classical music and they would both make calls on their mobile phones or take care of whatever business was at hand. When Dodi worked on his computer, Diana would often read. During this trip she was reading a book called *On Being Jewish*, a title I couldn't help noticing since she laid the book down with its cover facing me. Being Jewish myself, I wondered what made her choose it, although I never asked.

She read a lot, especially when Dodi was busy speaking with the captain or conducting other business, but one thing I noticed right away: She *never* read when Dodi was free. As soon as she saw that he wasn't doing anything else, she'd put her book away and turn to him. I found this unusual. I'd seen his previous girlfriends read or do whatever they wanted whenever they felt like it, no matter what he was doing. But the princess appeared to be much more interested in him than the others had been. When he was available, she was available. That's the way it always was.

Once the business chores were out of the way, they spent the rest of the day swimming, sunbathing, relaxing, talking and laughing. The hot Mediterranean sun seemed to melt all of their cares away, and they just let themselves go—gladly giving way to the relaxation, the sensuality and the pure enjoyment that a sun-and-sea holiday supplies in abundance. In the water, they were very playful, but not aggressive. They would often come together and put their arms around each other, kicking to stay afloat. Once, in a fun-loving mood, Diana even flung her leg over his shoulder. They reminded me of two kids.

She was more of a swimmer than he, and would often stay in longer, swimming the equivalent of several laps and sometimes performing some excellent dives. Then, once they'd climbed aboard and toweled off, they'd go back to reclining on the lounges, holding hands, rubbing each other with suntan lotion, laughing and, as always, carrying on their avid conversations. Many times, when I quietly looked in on them to see if their drinks needed refilling, her feet were resting in his lap, or his hand on hers.

I had never seen two people talk as much, or as intently, as they did! I sometimes found myself wondering what in the world they had to say to each other for hours on end! But now I think I know. These were two people who recognized themselves in each other, who really understood the other's hopes, dreams, wishes, fears and pain. Once each realized that the other understood and, more importantly, *cared*, the floodgates opened. Both were eager to reveal themselves, to get to know each other, and to gain the acceptance from each other that had eluded them in other relationships. In this atmosphere, every story from childhood on became a new revelation, a new piece of the puzzle. And neither could wait to see the picture that the puzzle would finally reveal.

I knew from experience that Dodi was an excellent listener, but the princess was every bit as good. Whenever he spoke, she gave him her full attention, leaning toward him and never interrupting. She nodded often, making a few short, sympathetic comments and encouraging him to tell her more. They were in the process of getting to know each other's souls—a process they took seriously and on which they spent much time. Often I'd feel guilty about interrupting these private moments, but it was my job to stand there, quiet and still, until my boss gave me a signal to stay or leave. Sometimes, after I'd been standing as quietly and invisibly as I could, either Dodi or Diana would laugh and say "OK, Rene, we see you," and then wave me away. It was a relief to be able to leave them in peace.

Their excitement at being together and their pleasure at just getting away from it all never seemed to diminish. Meanwhile, as the trip progressed, they seemed to get physically closer and closer. They were almost always touching each other in some little way—holding hands, rubbing shoulders, sitting with their legs right up next to each other, touching the other's arm or shoulder for emphasis when talking, or brushing a stray strand of hair out of the other's eyes. All of these signs of loving intimacy became more and more apparent as the days rolled by.

Lunch was served in the mid-afternoon, about three or four o'clock, usually consisting of green salad or seafood salad, with fish fillets or pasta with a seafood sauce. For dessert they often had *granita*, which is icy and fruity, like sorbet. We always covered the long, oval table with a beautiful, salmon-pink cloth and set their chairs at one corner, angled toward each other. After lunch, the princess and Dodi returned to the sundeck for more quiet time together. Then, at about six o'clock, I'd change from my shorts and shirt into my night uniform and go below to see what was available for dinner.

At around nine-thirty, after they'd showered and changed, Dodi and the princess would arrive together at the open-air salon. At the table on the left, I'd serve them cocktails and appetizers with, of course, caviar for the princess. As always, they'd pull their chairs together and lean closer, each with an elbow on the table. They'd then continue their intimate conversation in low tones, punctuated by an occasional sensual chuckle. He would sometimes touch her arm; she might put her hand on his.

Eventually, when they were ready to eat, they would move over to the other table, where I served the main meal. Dinner was enjoyed in the French way, meaning at a leisurely pace so the food and wine could be savored to the fullest. But for Dodi and Diana, the conversation remained the primary focus. Although I heard only fragments of what was said, because they talked in such low tones, I do know she spoke at length about her boys, whom she adored, and he told her a great many stories about the movie business. They usually continued talking long after the meal had ended and well into the morning hours. Then they would request a final cup of tea, always mint, after which Dodi would say, "Rene, thank you, you can retire now. We'll see you tomorrow for breakfast." I'd take my leave, giving them the privacy they obviously desired.

The food we had on the boat was absolutely exquisite. It included some of the most delicious fish, seafood salads and pasta salads I've ever tasted. We really couldn't have asked for a better chef than Christiano. But, like many fine chefs, he tended to prepare too much food.

One day Dodi said, "Rene, for lunch today we want only vegetables and salad, so try to explain that to Christiano. Nothing else, just vegetables and salad." He glanced inquiringly over at Diana, with whom he'd obviously just had a conversation on the subject. She smiled her approval.

"Mr. Fayed," I replied, "I will see him right away. How about if I set the table for a buffet and we have an assortment of six or seven vegetables, plus a salad with vinaigrette?"

"Absolutely. A great idea."

I made my way down to the galley and delivered the message to Christiano. He frowned and wanted to know why they didn't want something more elaborate, a reaction I expected. All chefs want to demonstrate their talents by creating the most spectacular dishes possible. A menu of vegetables and salad alone isn't much of a stretch for them.

"They just want to take a break from all the great food you've been giving them," I reassured him. "I think they'd rather eat very lightly during the day and have a nice dinner at night."

Christiano smiled resignedly. "OK," he said.

The final menu for lunch that day was an assortment of raw vegetables and five salads. That was about as restrained as Christiano was going to get!

Luckily my boss was happy with the menu and requested some music while they waited the hour or so it would take to prepare the food. I put on *The Three Tenors* and left them, the princess reading her book and Dodi aiming a sun reflector at his face.

Coming back to check on them fifteen minutes later, I coughed diplomatically before presenting myself. By then, she had put aside her reading and he his sun reflector. He lay on his back in a lounge chair and she was curled up beside him, her head in his lap. His left hand was buried in her beautiful blond hair, tenderly caressing her head. Both had their eyes closed and I knew better than to stay.

It was standard practice for the *Jonikal* to sail during the night so we would already be at our destination when we woke up the next morning. During our first night, we sailed from Nice to Corsica, a large island off the southeastern coast of France, anchoring some two to three hundred yards off a beach. It was a busy area, with lots of yachts at anchor, and many smaller boats either sailing or motoring here to there. The day was very hot, with almost no breeze. The water looked wonderfully blue and calm, the beach bright and inviting.

The princess had been leaning on the railing, looking at the coastline. She whirled around and said impulsively, "Dodi, why don't we swim to shore?"

As I've said before, my boss was not quite the swimmer that Diana was, but not wanting to spoil her fun, he said, "Great! I'll take the kayak."

Within minutes the two were in the water—the princess swimming her graceful yet powerful crawl, with Dodi, feet straight out in front of him in the kayak, paddling furiously in her wake. Unfortunately, they left without notifying their bodyguard. A bodyguard's job is to be near his clients at all times, keep photographers at bay and be on the lookout for any and all kinds of trouble. But Dodi and the princess took off so quickly that John, the security guard, was caught unaware. As soon as he realized they were gone, he raced to Luigi, the captain, requesting that a small boat be launched immediately. "Someone might recognize them," he said frantically. "I've got to be nearby in case they need me."

I went to the prow of the yacht, watching with a pair of binoculars as John and a crew member gunned their way in a small motorboat. Although there was no immediate danger and no threats of kidnapping, with a woman as famous as Diana, you simply never knew what might happen when people recognized her. And then, of course, all of us were concerned about the paparazzi.

We didn't think they could actually harm my boss and the princess; we just didn't want them ruining an otherwise glorious vacation.

Through my binoculars I could see the princess slicing quickly and cleanly through the water. At her side, Dodi matched her pace in the kayak and they made the three-hundred-yard trek in no time. Once they arrived at the beach, they stayed in the shallow water, splashing about and having fun. Nobody seemed to notice them. Within minutes, the bodyguards caught up with them and were hovering a discreet distance away.

After about twenty minutes of jumping waves and diving through some of them, then wading through the shallower water, holding hands, they returned to the *Jonikal* the same way they'd left it—he kayaking, she swimming. As they climbed the stairs and I handed them towels, I smiled broadly at the princess and discreetly applauded her for her excellent swimming of some six hundred yards. She returned my smile and said, "Rene, you swim. Why didn't you join us?"

The very idea surprised me. I would never have considered it.

"Because then, Madame," I replied, " I would not be serving you. I'll swim later on."

The fact was, Dodi made sure that I had time to swim every day so that I'd get my exercise. He knew that exercise was very important to me. Still, I appreciated the princess' attempt to include me. She was so thoughtful and such a "regular" person.

In the meantime, John, the security guard, had

made it back to the boat and was entreating Dodi to give him five or ten minutes' warning before taking any more spontaneous excursions. The paparazzi could appear and anything could happen, he explained. Dodi laughed. Not worried about the paparazzi, he didn't want the princess to feel as though any little move she made was going to be a big deal. Why couldn't she take a swim if she felt like it?

Later that day, after lunch, I took some fresh bottles of water up to the sundeck, where Dodi and the princess were spending the afternoon. I coughed as usual to warn them I was coming. Since they didn't say anything, I continued to climb the stairs. As I came up on deck, there was my boss on his stomach, with the princess sitting on his back, giving him a massage. Naturally, I felt a little embarrassed, but the princess looked over at me, so I figured I should say something.

Impulsively, I remarked, "Madame, you are taking my job!"

It was a joke, of course, but it was also true. One of the functions I performed was that of occasional masseur, if Dodi's neck or back began to hurt. The princess laughed good-naturedly, but Dodi raised his head and said in a mock-stern tone of voice, "Well, from now on, this part of the job doesn't belong to you anymore!"

We all laughed, and if I'd had any doubt that he was joking, it was dispelled that very night when he called me to his cabin to do "five minutes on my neck." I could tell that he wanted to talk. Sure enough, after a moment he said, "So, Rene, how do you find the princess so far? This is the first time you've had a chance to get to know her, since that time in Paris was very short."

"Mr. Fayed," I replied, "she is an absolutely wonderful person. She makes me feel so comfortable and she always treats me with the utmost respect. I have worked for you now for over seven years, and I've known all of your girlfriends, but I think she is the most special. And it's not just because she is a princess. It's the way she behaves. I can feel she's beautiful on the inside, not just the outside."

I wasn't saying this simply to be nice. I had, in the past, expressed concerns about more than one of his girlfriends. Often they seemed much more interested in his money and what he had to offer them than who he really was. It seemed apparent to me that many of the other women really didn't care about Dodi himself, what he wanted out of life, how he felt about things or what had hurt him in the past. They were there to get whatever they could out of him. But the princess really seemed to care. Now, as I looked down at his face, his head turned sideways, I could see him smiling in a satisfied way that I had never seen before. At last he seemed content; I felt he'd found something he'd been seeking all of his life.

"Mr. Fayed," I continued, "I've never met a princess before, but I don't think they're all like this one. She is beautiful, she has a great personality and she is a great human being."

"You're right, Rene," he said, beaming and shaking his head, as if in awe. "She's absolutely wonderful."

But little did we know that the paradise they were creating had already been invaded by a deadly snake. That afternoon, just about the time I'd come upon them during the massage, a photographer had snapped a telling picture of them embracing and kissing. Days later, the picture, which would be dubbed "The Kiss" by the press, appeared in London's *Sunday Mirror*, along with ten pages of other photos of the cruising couple. Soon their romance would no longer be private—it would belong to the masses.

But we on the boat were blissfully unaware of all this. That night, Debbie, Mary and I set the table, put out fresh flowers, dimmed the lights and lit candles everywhere. We conspired to make the evening as romantic as possible. Nature cooperated most graciously, and by the time I had served the champagne and appetizers, a large yellow moon had begun to rise and millions of stars dotted the inky black sky. At about ten-thirty, as the two of them sat on the couch sipping their predinner champagne, Dodi signaled me.

"Rene, I think we have the soundtrack of *The English Patient*," he said. "Diana would like to listen to it."

I slid the CD into place, pushed the button and the hauntingly beautiful music began to swell, spilling over the decks of the *Jonikal* and surrounding two people who were rapidly falling in love. Looking at them, I felt all was right with the world.

At that untimely moment, the telephone rang. While Dodi took the call inside, I stayed close to the princess.

"Rene, have you seen *The English Patient*?" she asked.

"Yes, Madame, I saw it twice. It was a wonderful movie, but I never noticed how beautiful the music was."

"Well, that's probably because the story is so beautiful and the music is in harmony with the images," she said. "You get totally absorbed in the movie, hearing but not noticing the music."

She put her feet up on the nearest chair and was reclining almost horizontally as she sipped her champagne. Seeing that she was enjoying the music, I quietly retreated, and after a few minutes, Dodi returned to her side. Later, when I went to find out what time they wanted to have dinner, I discovered that they were dancing, holding each other tightly. Her head was resting on his shoulder as they swayed gently to the music. I wanted to leave but I couldn't just turn around and go back; it was too obvious. So, instead, I stood stock-still, watching as invisibly as I could. It was one of the most loving, blissful moments I have ever witnessed. And no piece of music could have suited the two of them better. It was so full of longing, sadness, ecstasy and then fulfillment that I felt it perfectly mirrored their own relationship; it could have been written just for them. After about thirty seconds, I slipped away, went upstairs and told the girls, "I think dinner will be a little later than usual."

The following days continued in much the same vein. Dodi and the princess rose late in the morning, ate a leisurely breakfast, did a little work, read, sunbathed, swam and talked endlessly to each other. Dinner was a deliciously romantic affair that almost never began earlier than ten o'clock. As their love began to bloom, several of the staff accidentally walked in on them kissing, cuddling or sneaking an embrace, which was embarrassing to all involved. Although we took great pains to act as if we didn't notice anything out of the ordinary, secretly we were extremely curious as to how the relationship was going. Everything seemed to indicate that love had definitely arrived. We silently cheered.

As the romance progressed and Dodi began to seem more centered, more confident and more in control of his own destiny, he reaped rewards in many areas of his life, but none more dramatic than the improvement of his relationship with his father, which—although close—was sometimes marred by disagreements over Dodi's future. The biggest point of contention, as I understood it, was the son's desire to remain in the movie business vs. the father's wish to groom him to take over Harrods, the Ritz and the rest of the Fayed empire. We'd moved from California to France in the first place because of Mr. Al Fayed's desire to have Dodi take a more active role in the family business.

But Dodi's new sense of purpose and increased confidence sat well with his father. They spoke to each other on the phone daily, sometimes even several times a day. In his tone, I heard Dodi indicate both love and great respect for his father. It was a heartwarming thing to witness—a renewal of good feelings between father and son.

On August 5, the *Jonikal* headed toward Monaco, where there would be a fantastic fireworks display that night. Our destination each day was chosen (sometimes at the last minute) by my boss. Although we were often in a new place when we got up in the morning, Dodi also liked to take spontaneous little side trips during the day.

On a typical day, he would see Luigi right after breakfast, and the captain would show him where we were on the map, suggest possible destinations and calculate how long it would take to reach them. Based on this information, Dodi would decide where, if anywhere, we should go that day. On this particular occasion, he decided we should go to Monaco, which was a couple of hours away. We had lunch while under way, all of us keeping our eyes trained on the gorgeous coastline that drew closer by the minute. The weather was absolutely beautiful; nothing but sunshine and clear blue skies.

We anchored just outside the harbor at Monte Carlo, since Luigi was loath to be within its confines. Too many huge boats with everyone passing by and gawking at our yacht, he insisted. This famous ancient port was known for its steep, craggy cliffs, warm seas and sun-washed beaches. Naturally, once we'd dropped anchor, Dodi and the princess were anxious to go ashore. Sailing is great fun, but the urge to walk on land becomes irresistible after a few days on the water. John, the security guard, and I were chosen to accompany the couple, so the four of us piled into the tender and Luigi took us to a section of the harbor that didn't seem too busy.

Always the professional, John hopped ashore first and ran ahead a little way to make sure everything was OK before allowing us to get out of the boat. We were all dressed casually in T-shirts and shorts or pants, with the princess in jeans, a sweater, sunglasses and no makeup.

Dodi wanted to take a taxi, but taxis are not always easy to find in Monte Carlo. After waiting at the cab stand for five minutes, the princess suggested we walk. She was an avowed exercise buff and was eager to stretch her legs. Dodi warned her that they would have to walk up some pretty steep hills, but she didn't mind. "It's good exercise," she said laughingly, and encouraged him to get moving.

You'd think that going for a walk would be a simple matter, but it isn't if you're as famous and as sought-after as my boss and his new girlfriend were. We had to walk in a rather strange formation, with me in front acting as a "point," then Dodi and the princess together, holding hands, pressed tightly to each other's sides, and John in the rear to keep an eye on us all. My boss, of course, decided which route we would take. He would say, "Left, Rene" or "Go right, now." It made me laugh because I gave similar orders to his dogs, Romeo and Shoe, when I took them for a walk.

It was my first visit to this famous and beautiful city, but I didn't have much time to take it in as I was kept so busy scrutinizing the people coming toward us, watching for photographers, and turning left or right on command. To this day I'm not sure which streets we took or exactly where we wound up. I do know that we eventually found ourselves in an area where there were many boutiques and flower shops. When Dodi left us for a few seconds to check out something he'd seen in a window, I said to the princess, "The city is beautiful! It's my first time here." She smiled and replied, "Mine, too."

Just then I felt a little sorry for her, realizing that her entire adult life had been so highly organized that it probably left little time for fun. She'd spent so many years being told to do this and do that, go here and say that, following to the letter a predetermined schedule. How claustrophobic and held down she must have felt! How could she possibly enjoy visiting a city if she had to rush from one ribbon cutting to another, shake a thousand hands and give three speeches before flying off to the next city? It occurred to me that this might be the first time since her marriage to Prince Charles in 1981 that she'd been able to explore and enjoy a city with absolutely no plan or schedule.

When Dodi returned, we continued our walk (in formation, of course). We were pretty lucky that day; the tourists hardly bothered us. Of course, that didn't mean the princess could just walk around as freely as you or I. Even dressed very casually, wearing no makeup and sunglasses, she was still quite recognizable. She kept her head down when people passed, sometimes turning away and pretending to look at something in a shop window if they started staring. We knew some of the people recognized her because they were pointing and whispering to each other as they passed. That was all right and was even expected—we just hoped that no one would rush up and take a picture of her. Luckily, everyone seemed to be on their best behavior. Perhaps it was because the people of Monte Carlo were used to seeing celebrities, or they may have sympathized with Diana over her troubles with the paparazzi. Whatever the reason, everyone seemed content to respect her privacy. Everyone—except one German boy about eighteen years old.

Walking toward us on the other side of the street with his parents, he abruptly screamed and pointed at Diana. Clutching his camera, he pushed people out of the way and began to rush across the street. My heart pounded as I hurried toward him, holding up my hand and saying, "Please, no." I said it gently, with a smile, hoping he would back off as a favor. He stopped in his tracks, speaking German to me, undoubtedly asking if he could photograph the princess. Once again I smiled and said, "Please, no." He stared at me for a moment, then shrugged his shoulders and went back to his parents. I was flooded with relief as I returned to our small party. Fortunately, that was the extent of our trouble. Not too bad.

Our excursion completed, we returned to the *Jonikal,* where I had much work to do. That night we were having our only guests of the trip, Dodi's cousin Mudi and a male friend, who would be arriving in time to see the fireworks over Monaco. The four of them went up to the sundeck, the highest point of the yacht, from where they had a three hundred and sixty degree view. I was rushing around, trying to time the serving of the cocktails and appetizers so that I would also be able to watch the display from the deck. I thought I'd finally finished and was ready to enjoy the show when Dodi came to the little kitchen with a request. *Oh great*, I thought. Just when I was hoping to get a little time off to watch the fireworks! Dodi asked for a drink, and once I'd poured it and set it on a tray, he said, "Follow me." Then he led me up to the sundeck, where he and his guests had a spectacular view. Taking the drink from me, he said, "Don't rush back down, stay up here and watch with us." I was thrilled not only because I had a prime spot from which to watch the show, but because of his thoughtfulness in inviting me.

I remained with them for a full hour, watching the glorious lights shooting through the sky, and never once did the guests request anything, even though their glasses were empty. When I asked if they wanted more drinks, they all said, "No, no, watch the show."

The next morning, August 6, was the final day of the cruise. At one point, when I went to check on Dodi and the princess, she was alone. I felt she was a little sad and I asked if anything was wrong.

"We have to go back soon," she replied wistfully. "I've enjoyed this all so much, but I have other commitments this weekend." Then she told me about her upcoming trip to Bosnia, where she would work to eliminate the land mines that were maiming and killing both soldiers and civilians. With compassion in her voice, she spoke of the great pain and sorrow inflicted by those hidden devices.

"I'm sure, Madame, that your mere presence will make a big difference," I said, truly meaning it.

She looked at me and said, "I hope so, Rene. I really hope so."

And so my first cruise on the *Jonikal*, and the first trip "alone" for my boss and the princess, came to an end. They were to leave immediately for London, while I was going back to Paris. I, too, felt a little sad that this magical trip was over, and as I walked away from the princess, I said, "Madame, it was an absolutely wonderful pleasure and honor to take care of you. I hope to see you again."

She replied jubilantly, "You will, Rene!"

CHAPTER

5

Private Dinners, Quiet Moments

I returned to the Paris apartment suntanned, happy, a little weary and very aware that something big was happening. The change that had come over my boss since he'd met the princess was nothing short of miraculous. He was happier than I'd ever seen him, confident and focused. There was a direction in his life, and everything he did seemed to take on greater importance. He seemed at last to be a man with a mission. I was thrilled to see things working out so well for him.

Returning to the hustle-bustle and stifling summer heat of Paris was a bit of a culture shock but, as it turned out, I wasn't there for long. The day after I got back, Dodi called from London with some good news.

"Guess what, Rene?" his voice rang out joyfully. "You're going back to Los Angeles!"

"I'm what?" I said, not believing my own ears.

"I've just bought a house in Malibu. We're going to

move there, probably in September. You'll be able to go home to your family and friends!"

At last, after more than three years, I was hearing the words I'd been longing for! I could barely contain myself, I was so happy: Wanting to return to California had nothing to do with Dodi, the most wonderful boss anyone could have wanted. It was just that my heart was still in Los Angeles and I felt isolated and alone in Europe.

"Now, Rene," he continued, "here's what I want you to do. Fly to L.A. in a couple of days. Check out the house and see if we need anything there." Since I had been in charge of running his household in Beverly Hills for four years, he knew that I knew everything there was to know about his lifestyle. I'd be able to spot any additions or corrections that needed to be made so that everything would be to his liking.

Very excited, I packed a bag and took off on my "errand." The house, which had once been owned by actress Julie Andrews and her husband, director Blake Edwards, was located in Malibu's exclusive Paradise Cove. The beautiful five-acre estate included a hill, where the house was situated, plus grounds that extended all the way down to a private beach. The house, which was purchased completely furnished, was Mexican-style with a very open, airy feeling. There were almost no doors, and not too much furniture, giving the place a clean, simplistic style that was very refreshing. I guessed that this wide-open feeling was the main reason Dodi had purchased it. He told me he was planning to build a separate beach house, and that the beautiful glassed-in gym located on the hill would be converted to my quarters. I couldn't wait!

As I toured the home and the grounds, making note of what we would need to bring from Paris, I concluded that this was the perfect place for my boss. One of the few changes I suggested was the addition of new lighting to the patio ceiling, right near the barbecue, which I knew we'd be using a great deal.

When I got back to Paris, I called him in London. "Mr. Fayed, the house is absolutely wonderful. The princess is going to enjoy visiting."

"Good. I'm glad you like it," he replied softly. "I'm going to be in London for a little while longer, so I'll need you to come over tomorrow."

"All right, Mr. Fayed," I said. "I'll see you at Park Lane tomorrow."

In my three years of service to Dodi Fayed in Europe, I had hardly traveled at all. But now I was cruising off the south of France one day, flying to Los Angeles the next, zipping over to London after that. I probably did more traveling that summer than at any other time in my life. I liked it!

After quickly packing another bag, I took the chunnel to London and headed straight to the Fayeds' elegant Park Lane apartment/office complex. Here, in an eight-story building in one of the most fashionable sections of London, several Fayeds live and work, including Dodi's father, his uncle Salah and his wife, Dodi's cousin Mudi and his uncle Ali. From the street it's impossible to tell what's inside the building, since the ground-floor car dealership is the only thing visible. Dodi's apartment was on the fourth floor while his father, uncle Salah, uncle Ali and cousin Mudi had apartments elsewhere in the building. The seventh floor housed the offices from which the Fayed businesses were run, as well as a large kitchen that provided meals for the family.

With usual Fayed efficiency, I was greeted by someone who paid for the cab and gave me British currency. There was only one little slipup; they forgot to have someone on hand to let me into Dodi's apartment. Since I didn't have a key, I rang several times but no one answered. Finally I called my boss on my portable phone, and he came to the service door to let me in.

Dodi was alone in his apartment; in fact, most of the building was quiet that Sunday afternoon. He seemed preoccupied and I later found out why: That morning the *Sunday Mirror* had run "The Kiss" picture plus ten additional pages of photos of Dodi and the princess on the *Jonikal*. The huge sums of money paid for those photos ensured that the paparazzi would continue to harass the lovers. Any privacy they might enjoy in the future would be hard won.

Although he tried to hide it, Dodi was becoming worried, and from then on our security measures were stepped up. Plans were often changed quickly to throw the photographers off; we took circuitous routes and were always on the lookout for lurking paparazzi. We were never sure what was going to happen next.

The princess would be returning to London from Bosnia that day, and Dodi wanted to take her immediately to his father's estate in Oxted. She had visited the mansion prior to her first trip on the *Jonikal*. This time, however, she and Dodi would have the run of the place, since the Al Fayeds were off on vacation.

The gardens of the five-hundred-acre Oxted estate were phenomenal, especially in the summer, a horticulturist's delight with roses, weeping willow trees, hedges trimmed into giant mazes and beautifully manicured lawns that stretched as far as the eye could see. To take advantage of this unrivaled backdrop, on our first night I set a beautiful table at the edge of the garden, complete with solid silver flatware, fine porcelain china and priceless crystal goblets. This way the two lovers could dine while enjoying beautiful garden vistas that extended for perhaps a hundred yards on three sides. Behind them was the stately and elegant mansion. I was very proud of the exquisite setting I had helped create, but just as I began serving the cocktails, my boss said to me, "Rene, you know what?" My heart sank. I knew that he was about to stand our plans on their head.

He leaped out of his chair, assured the princess that he'd be right back and asked me to follow him. After leading me into the house, through the living room, out through another entrance and across a huge lawn to a secluded area about seventy-five yards away, we came upon a large white tent standing among the greenery. *What is this for?* I wondered as I circled the tent and peered inside. I could imagine medieval lords and ladies sitting there as they dined, or perhaps aristocrats watching the races at Ascot.

"We'll have our appetizers here," Dodi said decisively. "Then we'll eat back at the house, on the veranda."

This little change in plans, of course, triggered a flurry of activity. I hurried back to the manor, got a tablecloth, silverware, candles and glasses and rushed back to the tent to set up. I brought out the wine and hors d'oeuvres and before long, the white tent had been transformed into a romantic, candlelit hideaway. I understood why my boss wanted to change locations.

There were two lounge chairs in the tent, and Dodi pushed them together so that they could lie side by side. The princess looked lovely in a black trouser suit set off with a ruffled white silk blouse. When she removed her jacket, her blouse reminded me of the kind of shirt worn by a sixteenth-century poet, with wide sleeves gathered in a pouf at the shoulder and nipped in at the wrist with a narrow, ruffled band. In this outfit she blended perfectly with the surrounding setting—each as captivatingly romantic as the other.

I served the hors d'oeuvres and drinks, then discreetly disappeared, which was no small feat because it was a seventy-five-yard trek back to the house! But back and forth I'd go, every ten minutes or so. Surprisingly, they were very quiet that night and seemed content just to enjoy the silence and each other's company. The daylight gradually receded and the world took on a softer focus as they nibbled their caviar and sipped their drinks. She was on his right, her head sometimes resting on his shoulder and their fingers gently intertwined as they watched the pink sky fade to coral, then lavender, then deep, dark blue. Later, she moved her chair around so her head rested in his lap. They stayed there for a long time, wrapped in a cocoon of contentment and undisturbed peace.

At about ten o'clock they came back to the veranda for a barbecue. Dodi had arranged this with me in advance, having told the princess, "You should try Rene's chicken burgers and his salmon tartare. They're fantastic!"

While my responsibilities only occasionally included cooking, I did have a few specialties I could whip up, and these were two that Dodi especially liked. Since they were my original recipes, I needed to spend time with the chef to tell him how to make them. I divided my time between making the long trek from the house to the tent, and instructing Cheesy, the chef, in the fine art of making salmon tartare and chicken burgers. (We called him Cheesy because his real name was so difficult to pronounce. I think he was from India.) Cheesy also whipped up a little salad, got out some sausages and stoked the barbecue, so that all was in readiness when the couple came back for dinner. The chicken burgers and sausages were sizzling away, their fragrant, smoky aroma filling the air.

As they settled themselves at the table, I noticed that the two were no longer content with silence, but had begun to speak softly to each other. The tone of their conversation was both urgent and intimate as they looked into each other's eyes, apparently revealing what was in their hearts. They were so wrapped up in each other and their conversation, they barely noticed me.

As I served the meal and later took away the plates, Dodi and the princess continued talking nonstop. And long after the ice cream was finished, long after I had cleared the table and served the wine, long after the candles had burned low, they remained deeply engrossed in their conversation. It was absolutely clear to me then that they had fallen head over heels in love.

Finally, at midnight, Dodi and the princess finished their barbecue and prepared to retire to their rooms. He requested cognac, his favorite Cohiba Borrusto cigar and a half glass of wine for Diana. As soon as I served them, they picked up their drinks and walked arm in arm into the house. I sighed as I watched them go, thinking that there is simply nothing better on earth than true love.

Moments later, as I was returning to the table to take away the candles and the linens, I heard beautiful music coming from their suites on the second floor—rich, gorgeous piano music, played with sensitivity and warmth. I assumed it was a CD that I'd never heard before. Listening appreciatively from the living room on the first floor, I wondered what its title was, making a mental note to find out the next day. I wanted a copy for myself.

The next morning I was in the kitchen with the rest of the staff, waiting for my boss and the princess to arise. Then Dodi phoned, saying, "Rene, please bring the coffee, as usual. The one the princess likes and for me, an espresso."

"Yes, sir, I'll bring them up right away."

There was one small problem—I didn't know which room he called me from. When they had arrived, she had taken the master bedroom and he one of the others, but who knew where they ended up? I put the coffees on a tray and went straight to Dodi's bedroom. When no one answered my knock, I tried a second time, then went to the princess' room and knocked softly on her door. This time the door was answered. Dodi opened it just partway, grabbed the coffees and said quickly, "Thank you. You can go." The door slammed shut on their privacy.

Later, when the two came down to breakfast, I was about to ask the princess for the name of the CD they were playing the night before, when something stopped me. Instead, I said quite impulsively, "Madame, was that *you* playing the piano last night?"

She shyly tilted her head to the side and smilingly replied, "Yes."

I was taken aback for a moment, so surprised that I'd been right. When I finally found my voice, I exclaimed, "It was beautiful! You play beautifully!"

"Thank you," she replied modestly. "Everyone in my family plays."

That was all she said about it, but I liked to imagine the scene that I had only witnessed by ear. She, seated majestically at the piano on the landing, playing that gorgeous music for Dodi while he relaxed on the couch, sipping his cognac and puffing on his cigar. I could just imagine the look of contentment he must have had on his face, with that little smile playing about his lips. Just a simple, quiet evening at home for a loving, happy couple—a respite from their worldly cares. This kind of evening—one that so many of us would take for granted—was a rare treat for them.

We stayed at Oxted only that one night, then returned to London. But a couple of days later, we repeated the trip. Obviously, it was a great deal easier for Dodi and the princess to enjoy their privacy at the countryside mansion than in London, where the paparazzi had staked out their homes.

This time when they arrived, Diana had a little gift for Edna, the woman who ran the household. In her late sixties, Edna had been with the Al Fayed family for more than thirty years, and Dodi had obviously mentioned something to Diana about Edna's devoted service. Edna practically trembled with excitement as she opened the gift, a beautiful, egg-shaped ornament. She was genuinely touched by the princess' thoughtfulness and proudly showed the gift to all of us. It was just like Diana to do something like that, honoring a faithful, trusted servant with a thoughtful gift, even though she'd met her only once before.

Dodi and the princess had so enjoyed "camping out" that they repeated the experience—hors d'oeuvres and drinks in the tent, dinner on the veranda. Then, the following day, the two of them took the helicopter and went off on some sort of adventure. I wasn't told where they were going (in fact, neither was the helicopter pilot until they were airborne!), but later I found out that Diana wanted Dodi to meet her adviser, Rita Rogers, in

Derbyshire. The princess enjoyed astrology and evidently wanted to find out if the future was going to be bright for her and her new love.

The next day Dodi announced that it was time to leave his father's mansion and head back to London, so Trevor Rees-Jones (Dodi's favorite bodyguard), the chauffeur and I scurried around, loading luggage into the trunk of the Aston Martin and the back of the van. Although Dodi and Diana had intended to travel in the luxurious Aston Martin, at the last minute they decided to ride in the van to throw off the paparazzi. So Trevor and I hopped into the luxury car and drove off down the long driveway, followed by the van. (Later on, the princess asked me, with a twinkle in her eye, "How did you like riding in *my* car?" and we both laughed.)

As we drew closer to the gates of the mansion we knew the paparazzi would be waiting for us. Although they weren't legally allowed on the grounds, they could (and did) wait at the entrance of the mansion's private driveway. We all dreaded what would happen once we reached the gates and turned onto the public road. Would they mob the car? Follow us on their motorcycles? Ride right up alongside us, flashing their cameras into our windows? Or, worst of all, get in front of us and slam on the brakes, forcing us to stop?

As we approached the road, we could see a pack of maybe ten paparazzi. There was nothing to do but slowly make our way through. However, as luck would have it, a huge truck had pulled up and blocked the paparazzi vehicles, so we turned onto the road and sped away. I have no idea if that was a planned maneuver; if so, it was brilliant. If not, we were incredibly lucky. Trevor and I hooted joyously as we zipped off with the van behind us, leaving the paparazzi in the dust.

We'd shaken our pursuers only temporarily, of course. They all had portable phones and we knew they'd call their friends, who would be waiting for us ahead. Luckily, our security personnel had a different car waiting for us at a prearranged spot. Diana quickly switched vehicles and roared off into the distance. We'd successfully managed to evade the press—this time.

When we got back to Park Lane, Dodi informed me that the princess would be joining him for dinner that night. As is the case with most new lovers, they obviously couldn't bear to be apart.

"Tonight," he told me, "I'd like to begin with cocktails in my office."

His office in the London apartment was a beautifully appointed room filled with pictures of himself with scores of famous people—movie stars, heads of state and other celebrities. Framed pictures covered the desk and several tables. It was an impressive sight.

They would have drinks at a small coffee table in front of the couch, and dinner would be served at the massive table in the dining room. It was always covered with a white cloth, and two silver pieces sat in the center, one for fruit, the other for flowers. I automatically put the two settings at the end of the table, at right angles to each other, so they would be close together. Dinner had to be finished by ten, Dodi instructed, because he was planning on taking the princess to a private screening of *Air Force One*.

"Oh, Rene, you are coming with us to the movie," he said.

I was taken aback. Why would these two lovers want me to tag along? He had invited me to screenings before, but I never wanted him to think that he had to ask me along just to be nice, so I tried to give him an out.

"Oh, thank you, sir, but no. I have much to do here."

"Oh, come on, Rene," he cajoled. "It will be fun."

For some reason, it seemed that he really wanted me to go. If that was the case, why not?

"Well then, thank you very much, sir. I would love to," I replied.

Conference over, I took my leave and began preparations for the evening. At the Park Lane complex we had one chef in a central kitchen to cook for everyone. In that way, it was something like a hotel. We had a small refrigerator in the apartment stocked with snacks and drinks, but all food was prepared in the kitchen and sent over. All you had to do was pick up the phone and order what you wanted.

I preferred to talk to the kitchen personnel face-to-face, so I took the elevator from Dodi's fourth floor apartment to the seventh floor. There, I told the chef, "Mr. Fayed is having one guest for dinner tonight. We'd like some cracked crab for an appetizer, then fish, a little salad, some steamed vegetables and rice. Before dinner we'd like caviar and toast, and for dessert, ice cream. We also need nuts for the coffee table and dinner should be served about nine o'clock."

This was only my second trip to the Park Lane apartment, so the kitchen staff didn't know me well. Still, they were very polite and cooperative, and I knew they would follow my instructions exactly.

When the princess arrived, looking wonderful in a cream-colored jacket with matching pants, Dodi greeted her at the door, where they exchanged a loving embrace. She caught sight of me right away, giving me a friendly little wave before Dodi spirited her off to his office.

I brought them each a small glass of wine; then, as usual, I retreated, checking back every ten minutes to see if they wanted anything. During one of my visits, wine bottle in hand, I slipped quietly into the office and saw that they were exchanging gifts. They were beaming at each other as Diana sat on the couch, Dodi across from her on a plush chair. She opened hers first, squealing with delight when she uncovered a beautifully framed photograph of Dodi. When he opened his, an exquisite picture of her in a tasteful silver frame, he simply melted. The look on his face told it all—he was utterly in love. They set their pictures upon a small table and admired them. Not wanting to interrupt this tender moment, I had been standing like a statue the entire time, wine bottle in hand. Finally, when it seemed safe to move, I refilled the drinks and beat a hasty retreat.

At nine they were ready to eat, so I hurried upstairs to the kitchen to inform the cook. Everything was in place for a smooth dinner service. But when I went back to the office to tell Dodi it was time to move to the dining room, he smiled and said, "Rene, you know what?"

Here we go again, I thought. Diana, who knew what he was about to say, smiled at me apologetically as I waited for the bad news.

"We are very comfortable here," Dodi announced. "So comfortable that we would like to dine right here."

Oh boy. How was I supposed to lay out a full service of china, silver and crystal, plus the food, on this tiny coffee table?

"But Mr. Fayed," I said. "Where will we put the food? There's barely room for the plates on this little table!"

"Don't worry," he replied, smiling mischievously. "We'll put the plates on our laps!"

As I've mentioned before, one of the most difficult aspects of my job was dealing with the last-minute changes. This time it was even worse because we were working under pressure—my boss wanted to leave in about an hour for the screening. But I kept my cool, quickly hunted up a little tablecloth to cover the coffee table, then transferred the silverware, salt and pepper, crystalware and everything else they would need. I served the food as graciously as possible under the circumstances, doubting that they would be happy with their sudden change in plans. I was wrong. They sat there in Dodi's office, balancing their plates on their laps, as happy as two clams, smiling, laughing and catching up on the latest gossip. But there was no time to linger. As soon as they'd eaten, we grabbed our jackets and took off for the movie theater, leaving the dirty plates and platters of food where they were.

In the lobby we met Trevor and another security guard I didn't know, then quickly walked to the garage. By then, of course, the Diana and Dodi romance was worldwide news so the paparazzi were dying to get a picture of the two doing *anything*, even just walking down the street. We would have to exercise extreme precautions if we were to keep the annoyance to a minimum.

When the garage door opened, I saw at least a dozen paparazzi waiting to pounce. As we moved slowly forward, they rushed toward us en masse, cameras flashing blindingly. Although I felt uncomfortable, I was not afraid. After all, what could a bunch of paparazzi do to us? I turned to see how Dodi and the princess were reacting and found them lying down, almost on the floor of the car, giggling conspiratorially as they tried to escape the prying eyes and glaring flashes.

Over the roar, I heard one of the photographers say, "Nobody's there."

But another insisted, "Yes, yes, I see something."

With the determination of sharks who have tasted blood, they doggedly snapped away. It actually made me laugh. What were they going to do tomorrow with all those pictures of Trevor and me? Perhaps the two of us would appear in the tabloids!

With a second car following us, we performed a few evasive maneuvers to make sure no one was able to tail us. Trevor and the other driver kept in constant contact by walkie-talkie, exchanging information on cars that might be following us, discussing route changes to confuse the paparazzi. Luckily, we made it to the theater with no mishaps.

Once there, Trevor hopped out to check the area. It was dark and very quiet—no traffic, no one walking by. "Come quickly," Trevor said, ushering us out of the van. He hurried ahead to open the door to the theater and let us in, then dashed out to park the car. The other security guard stayed in his car and waited for us.

Dodi, who knew the place well, led us first to the projection room, where he gave instructions, then to the hundred-seat theater. The two lovers settled in the front row, she to his right. In accordance with Dodi's instructions, Trevor sat on the right side about halfway back, and I sat in the middle of the back row. It was impossible not to notice Dodi and Diana, since they were right in my line of vision, silhouetted on the screen. Off and on during the movie, I saw them looking at each other, sometimes talking; once in a while she would lean her head on his shoulder. They were like any happy moviegoing couple.

Air Force One is a thrilling action-adventure in which Harrison Ford plays the president of the United States, who personally defeats the nasty skyjackers who kidnap and threaten to kill him, his wife and his daughter. After the electrifying climax, in which Ford, his family and the remaining "good guys" switch planes in midair, our small audience was cheering. The princess, in particular, really loved it. As we walked up the aisle toward the exit, our projectionist leaned out and yelled, "God bless America!" The princess yelled, "Yeah!" and we all agreed.

Our high spirits were quickly dampened as we neared the theater exit. Back to reality. Had the paparazzi figured out where we had gone, and called the others? Would they be poised and ready to jump out at us as soon as the door swung open? Trevor had left earlier to get the van, and the rest of us huddled closer together as I tentatively pushed open the heavy door. To our great relief, the street was nearly empty and the van was idling just a few feet away, with Trevor standing by. We hurried out, piled in and took off.

Our first stop was Kensington Palace, Diana's home. As we drove up to the gates, a guard came out to ask us our business.

"Good evening, sir," he said formally to Trevor.

The princess called out from the backseat, "It's me! It's OK!"

The guard was taken aback. Squinting into the car, he recognized Princess Diana and was immediately apologetic.

"Oh, I'm terribly sorry, Ma'am."

"It's all right," she said cheerily. "They're just dropping me off."

"Very good, Ma'am," he said, opening the gate immediately. We sailed through and headed toward her apartments. The guard at the gate must have alerted the princess' butler that she was on her way, because he was standing in the lighted doorway waiting for her. She hopped out and brought him back to the car, where she introduced him not only to Dodi, but also to Trevor and me. This was just one more small indication of the kind of person she was—so careful to include others and make them feel like friends, rather than servants.

"Good night, all!" she called to us, turning to walk back toward the palace with her butler. We watched her for a few seconds, then drove back to Park Lane in silence.

Dodi and I talked about the movie as we rode the small, European-style elevator up to his apartment. Then, all at once, a thought occurred to me and it burst out of my mouth before I knew I was saying it.

"Do you realize, Mr. Fayed," I said, "that if things keep going as well as they are now, you may become the stepfather of the future king of England?"

I normally didn't ask personal questions or volunteer personal remarks like that, but my mouth seemed to have a will of its own that night. I was relieved when he laughed and nodded, which gave me the courage to continue.

"You know, of course, that you will have to say goodbye to your private life. Your privacy will be almost nonexistent."

His smile dimmed slightly. "I know."

The elevator opened at our floor. He went to his bedroom, where I served him some Evian.

"Thank you, Rene," he said. "You can retire for the night now."

"Oh no, sir," I said, thinking of the dirty plates from dinner. "I need to clean up the office."

"Never mind about that," he said, waving his hand dismissively. "Go to bed and the maid can take care of it in the morning."

“Thank you, Mr. Fayed,” I said, going off to clean the office anyway.

Later, as I retired to my quarters, I thought about how very kind Dodi always was to me. As I prepared for bed, I reflected on all that had happened that night—the running from the paparazzi, the movie, the trip to Kensington Palace, meeting Diana’s butler. But the most amazing thing was that my boss had confirmed that he’d at least *thought* about the possibility of marrying the princess. I wondered what the future would hold for him, for them and for me. As I went to sleep that night, I was sure that someday I would have plenty of glorious stories to tell my sons and grandchildren.

CHAPTER

6

Love on the High Seas

A few days later, I returned to the Paris apartment and had some time to myself while my boss attended to business in Los Angeles and Diana went off on a pre-arranged cruise of the Greek isles with a female friend. I was aware that as soon as Dodi came back, we'd be taking another excursion on the *Jonikal* with the princess. However, this time we were scheduled for a longer (ten-day) cruise.

On August 21, I flew to Nice with Dodi's regular masseuse, Myraiah, who would be providing the two lovers with daily massages. Referred to him by movie director Richard Donner, she had been giving my boss massages for the past four or five years. After his first session with her, he was awestruck. He said to me, "Rene, I've never had that kind of massage in my entire life." Because of chronic problems with his neck and back, he often took Myraiah with him on business trips and vacations.

Myraiah and I took a cab from Nice airport to St. Laurent-du-Var harbor, where the tender was waiting for us. The *Jonikal* itself had not yet arrived, but after we waited around for about an hour, it appeared in the distance, a huge, white form, its prow slicing through the water. What a gorgeous vessel it was!

As we climbed aboard I thought how good it felt to be back, associating the boat with such happy times. I went to my cabin, quickly unpacked and changed into my night uniform before Dodi and Diana arrived.

At about half past eight, the tender motored up to the *Jonikal* and crew members helped Diana and Dodi aboard. They were tired, having flown directly from London but, as always, happy to be together in their own private world. The princess greeted me graciously, shaking my hand and smiling.

"Rene," she said warmly, "it's so nice to see you again."

"Madame," I replied, "it is the same for me." And I meant it.

They had an early dinner, then retired to the living room to relax and sip their mint tea. This first night of the trip was a quiet, warmly intimate one. They had brought each other lover's gifts, which they were just beginning to open as I came around to check on them. Snuggled together on the living room couch, they were admiring his gift to her—a gorgeous gold-and-black bracelet. She exclaimed, "Oh, this is beautiful!" and immediately put it on her wrist. I heard him reply softly, "But it pales in comparison to you." I could see that this reply caught her fancy, because she stopped for a moment, turned and looked into his eyes. Then she laughed softly and murmured, "Oh, that's clever," giving him a warm hug and a kiss on the cheek.

During this trip we cruised first to Monaco, then spent our time primarily off the coast of the French island of Corsica and the Italian island of Sardinia. Unfortunately, we didn't enjoy the peace and quiet of our former trip, for we were constantly dogged by the paparazzi. By now, as I mentioned earlier, pictures of Diana and Dodi splashing about and embracing during the first cruise (including the famous "Kiss" photo) had been published worldwide, earning the photographers record-breaking sums of money, reportedly in the millions. As a result, everybody was now on the trail of the most famous woman in the world as she embarked on her first major postdivorce love affair. Consumed by the idea of snapping photos that could make them rich, the paparazzi stalked us day and night.

A boatload of them trailed in our wake no matter where we went, shooting photographs of Dodi and the princess with telephoto lenses. If the two dared to go for a swim, paparazzi surrounded them like hungry sharks, snapping away constantly. Their aggressiveness was truly intimidating, sometimes even frightening and always irritating. Even we crew members felt pursued, although they certainly weren't after us. Still, we were angry at the ever-present intrusion.

Trevor and Alexander "Kes" Wingfield, the bodyguards during this trip, spent the bulk of their days peering through binoculars at the paparazzi boat and any others nearby to determine who might be watching us. Although pleasant, Kes was very quiet and reserved. With the binoculars he always seemed to wear around his neck, he constantly searched for potential problems. Sometimes I would hear him say, "Trevor, on the right there's a big camera pointed toward us." It was obvious that our whereabouts were well known, and the *Jonikal* itself wasn't exactly easy to hide. Massive in size, with the name written clearly on either side, it announced itself wherever it went.

In spite of the intrusion, the two lovers enjoyed themselves immensely, quickly falling into the routine they had established previously. After a late breakfast they would take care of their personal business, then they might take the Jet Ski for a spin, go for a swim or just relax together in the sun.

Following a leisurely lunch they'd swim, lie in the sun and read, but mostly just sit or lie together, talking and laughing quietly. I often came upon them holding hands, cuddling and murmuring softly to each other. Although they had always conversed in low, quiet tones, their conversations now seemed to have become so intimate that they spoke almost in whispers, punctuated by lots of muffled laughter.

As before, dinner was an intimate, candlelit affair in the open-air salon at the back of the vessel. Sometimes they would eat early so they could take the tender ashore and walk around, but usually they just relaxed and took their time over dinner.

On that first day, we anchored at the far reaches of

the harbor at Monte Carlo, as was our custom, for maximum protection and privacy. Around five in the afternoon, I decided to take a break from my work and soak up the picturesque view of the harbor and the rocky cliffs rising steeply above it. Marveling at yet another glorious, sun-drenched jewel of a day on the Cote d'Azur, I pulled up a chair on the walkway of the second deck, right by the little kitchen. To enhance my enjoyment, I lit up one of the cheap, two-dollar cigars that I like so much and began to puff away.

Catching a movement out of the corner of my eye, I noticed the princess, perhaps thirty yards away, near where the tenders and Jet Skis were stored. She was doing her exercises, and when she saw me sitting there, puffing on my cigar, a playful look crossed her face. Smiling, she began pantomiming my cigar smoking, with big, exaggerated gestures, working them into her exercises. She puffed on her imaginary cigar, then swooped down to touch her toes, came back up, took another puff, then swooped down again. She captured my posture, the way I held my cigar, the way I puffed and blew out the smoke. She was very good—I found myself laughing out loud! I applauded her. She smiled, gave a little bow and left. I went back to my cigar, again reminded that the princess was just a person, like all the rest of us...only maybe with a gift for comedy!

That evening, after enjoying a day of sunning and swimming and an early dinner, Dodi and Diana decided to go ashore for some window shopping in Monte Carlo. Spending time on the *Jonikal* was wonderful—

so relaxing, luxurious and intimate—but land beckoned, providing an opportunity to stretch one's legs.

Dodi asked me to accompany them, along with Kes and Trevor, so the five of us piled aboard the tender, with Luigi at the helm. On our last trip to Monte Carlo, we had gone ashore during the day, but this time night was falling and the glittering lights of the gorgeous old city greeted us like a brightly lit Christmas tree. As we neared land, Dodi asked Luigi to find a quiet area, one where there wouldn't be too many people. They were hoping against hope that Diana and Dodi would not be noticed.

Luigi took us to the same quiet spot where we had docked the last time. We climbed the stairs to the sidewalk and assumed our former positions. At times it seemed almost like marching in military formation! But, of course, it was absolutely necessary for security's sake.

We had barely finished climbing the stairs from the harbor to the promenade when the princess made a little sound, as if she was alarmed. I wheeled around to see her pointing to a man lurking near some bushes up ahead.

"It's one of the paparazzi," she said anxiously. "I recognize him, he's bad news. Let's go back."

This was unusual behavior for her. She normally just ignored the photographers. But for some reason, this one really bothered her. We immediately made an about-face and started walking back rapidly toward the tender. Looking over my shoulder, I was alarmed to see that the man had taken out his cellular phone, obviously reporting our whereabouts to his friends. I was sure they would soon descend on us like a swarm of locusts. We walked faster, then broke into a run. Racing down the dock, we leaped into the tender and roared off, leaving the journalist in a cloud of exhaust fumes.

As we sped away, I thought about how unfair it all was. These two people simply wanted to take a stroll in the evening like anybody else, and yet they were mercilessly hunted and stalked as if they were animals.

Dodi urged Luigi on to the opposite side of the harbor. "Hurry," he implored, looking behind him at the receding figure on the dock. "Let's get ashore before they have time to follow us."

We sped across the harbor to the other side, jumped ashore and, again in formation, hustled onto the sidewalk, trying to lose ourselves in the crowd. When at last we felt certain that we weren't being followed, that we'd finally shaken them, we breathed a collective sigh of relief. Then the princess started to giggle. We all looked at one another for a moment as her mirth began to spread, and soon we were all laughing. Was it the ridiculousness of the situation or just plain, old-fashioned hysteria? Who knew? All we were certain of was that we'd escaped our pursuers temporarily, and now we were filled with glee. It felt good to win a battle, even a small one, in our ongoing war with the paparazzi.

Spirits high, we strolled through the streets of Monte Carlo that warm summer evening. Being August, it was the height of the tourist season and throngs of people crowded the sidewalks, lending an atmosphere of excitement and jubilation. We walked and window-shopped for perhaps two hours, looking mostly at the displays of clothing, jewelry and items that might interest Diana's sons. The lovers enjoyed every minute of it. But when it was finally time to meet Luigi with the tender, Dodi wasn't quite sure how to get to our designated meeting place. We started walking up and down streets, turning this way and that, acting as if we knew what we were doing, but the truth of the matter was we were lost. Cheerful as always, Dodi kept saying, "We'll be there soon. Soon."

The princess didn't seem to mind that we didn't know where we were going. She just wanted to pick up the pace, to get a little more exercise before returning to the boat.

"Come on, Dodi," she urged. "Faster! It's good for you."

Finally, after about thirty minutes of wandering around, we stumbled into a hotel on the beach, thirsty and tired. I asked the manager if we could have our tender pick us up at their little unlighted pier and, sympathetic to our plight, he said OK. Dodi called Luigi to tell him to come and get us and, luckily, Luigi seemed to know exactly where we were. (Later, when I asked him how he could possibly have found us in such darkness, he simply replied, "That's why I'm the captain.")

At midnight, we climbed aboard the *Jonikal* once again, tired but happy. Our promenade through Monte Carlo had been fun, despite the little excitement with the paparazzi. Dodi and Diana retired to the main living room as I brought their mint tea. The princess asked me if we had any cookies, so I went to fetch them and when I returned, the lovers were lying together on the couch, sides pressed together, hands intertwined. They were the picture of bliss.

Later, when I went to check, he was sitting up and she was lying down with her head in his lap, the cookies and tea untouched. When I checked one more time, at about one o'clock in the morning, they were gone.

Life on the *Jonikal* took on an easygoing rhythm of its own, with the quietest moments of the day always occurring after lunch. It was during this time that I was most likely to have a conversation with the princess; Dodi would be conducting business on the phone or computer, and she would be alone.

One afternoon I was strolling on the deck, just cruising around, making sure everything was OK. Diana was chatting on her portable phone, with one leg up on the railing, as if it were a ballet barre. She was leaning in toward her leg, stretching it. When she caught sight of me, I was about ten yards away and I gave her the OK sign to compliment her on her flexibility. She ended her phone call, took her leg off the railing and said, "Rene, do you work out?"

"Yes, Madame," I replied. "Since the age of thirteen. I don't work out because I have to, but because I enjoy it. It's like a drug to me; something that I have to do almost every day, if I can."

"Me too," she said. "When I'm in London, I never miss a single day."

We started talking about exercise; then somehow the conversation turned to food. I found myself telling her how important it was to eat fruit every day, particularly in the morning, after which you should wait twenty minutes before having anything else. (I had read some health books, particularly one called *Fit For Life*.) I talked about always eating plenty of vegetables, fruits and grains, while eating less meat, dairy products and fat.

I discovered that Diana didn't reserve her excellent listening skills just for Dodi; she also gave me her full attention, as I believe she would have done for anyone who spoke to her. Listening closely to my diatribe, she acted as if I were telling her something she never heard before, which, of course, couldn't be true. Anyone who was as health- and body-conscious as she surely knew all about proper nutrition. Still, she listened very politely and diplomatically. Suddenly an embarrassing thought hit me: *Oh my God, here I am pontificating! She probably already knows all of this.* I quickly asked if she needed anything, and then made myself scarce, hoping she didn't think I was tiresome. She must not have been put off, though, because we had several chats after that, just the two of us, and she always seemed interested in my point of view.

I particularly remember one afternoon when Diana was by herself on the sundeck and I went up to check on her. I, of course, would never begin a personal conversation with either the princess or my boss, but if they asked me a question, I always answered honestly and completely. And sometimes, when the princess and I were alone, she would ask me about myself.

On this sunny, golden afternoon, she looked up at me and asked, "Rene, are you married? Do you have a family?"

"Well, Madame, I am not married at this time, but I have been married twice and have two sons."

This caught her interest immediately and she began to ask me many questions: how it felt to lose a marriage, what my boys were like, how they got along with their stepmother, how they handled the divorces, how I dealt with custody and visitation and, particularly, what my relationship with the boys was like. Interestingly, she didn't reveal much about herself during this conversation, just asked questions designed to get me to talk. She was obviously very curious about how other families dealt with divorce and the subsequent raising of children.

She seemed cheered when I told her that despite our family troubles and separations, I manage to maintain a close relationship with my sons. "When each of my sons turned ten years old, I took him aside and said, 'I want to be not only your father, but your best friend. If you have any trouble, I want you to come to me as you would a friend. I will always be there to help you.' As it's turned out," I added, "that's exactly the relationship I have with both of them—best friends."

The princess smiled and nodded understandingly. Putting a friendly hand on my arm, she said, "That's wonderful. I'm so glad things have worked out well."

I remember another time when she wanted to take a swim while Dodi was working on his computer.

"Rene," she said, "could you please come and watch me?"

"Of course, Madame," I replied.

I brought a towel and sat on the steps of the ladder leading down to the water. She did a perfect jackknife and swam about thirty yards. After swimming around for ten minutes, she came back abruptly and grabbed on to the edge of the ladder, panting.

"Rene," she gasped, "I think there's a boat out there with a big telephoto lens. Maybe I should get out now."

I knew she wasn't ready to get out; she really wanted to continue her swimming to get some more exercise.

"Madame," I said, "by now they've probably already taken all the pictures they want. One more or one less, what difference will it make? I know you enjoy swimming. Let them take pictures; you enjoy."

She looked up at me and smiled.

"You know what, Rene?" she said. "You're right."

She swam for at least another ten minutes, then dove off the platform a good six or seven times. When at last she finished, I handed her the towel, smiling proudly at her for her courage. As she settled herself on the deck, she said, "That was great, Rene. Thanks for the encouragement! I really needed it."

The days continued to blend together, a festival of sunshine, seawater, candlelight and starlight, one nearly indistinguishable from another. On the *Jonikal*, we never knew or cared what day it was—it was all just a relaxed and happy blur. But occasionally, when guests came to dinner, we experienced a break in routine and an infusion of new energy. It was during one of those warm August nights, somewhere in the middle of the trip, that we were visited by Dodi's uncle Salah, his aunt Adriana and a couple from Saudi Arabia.

I was very familiar with Salah, who was Mohammed Al Fayed's brother, and his wife, Adriana, both of whom I had met three years earlier in Gstaad. Uncle Salah's chalet was right across the street, and I found him and his family, like all the Fayeds, to be warm and gracious. Salah and Adriana also had an apartment at the Park Lane residence and often rendezvoused with the *Jonikal* when they were cruising on their own yacht, the *Ramses*. I had seen them many times. This night would be a special one, however, since it was, I believe, the first time that Dodi's aunt and uncle were to meet Diana.

From the moment the guests arrived, the evening progressed wonderfully. The Fayed family is surprisingly unpretentious; their easygoing attitude and sense of fun is contagious. Right away, everyone was laughing and telling jokes, almost as if they'd known each other for years. But underneath all the gaiety, one very big change had occurred that evening. Diana, who had always played the part of a guest on the yacht, took over the role of hostess, welcoming the guests, making sure they were attended to and seeing that no one was left out of the conversation. She had undergone a subtle but important metamorphosis, becoming "the lady of the house." To me, this spoke volumes about the state of their relationship.

Dinner was served at the main dining table, with Dodi, the princess and the wife of the Saudi man on one side, and Uncle Salah, Aunt Adriana and the Saudi man on the other side.

The atmosphere that evening was full of fun and energy, with nonstop jokes and conversation. The attention, of course, focused mainly on Diana, who was the star of the evening, although she never monopolized the conversation. Instead, she made it a point to include everyone else and make the guests feel at home.

Through it all, I noticed that whenever she and Dodi weren't eating, they were holding hands, with their hands sometimes resting in his lap, sometimes in hers. It was as if they were silently telling each other, "No matter how many people may be with us, I want to be close to you. You matter most to me."

After dinner, dessert and coffee, they all spent another forty-five minutes enjoying each other's company before a speedboat arrived to take the Saudi Arabian guests away. Uncle Salah and Aunt Adriana stayed thirty minutes longer, sharing family time together. Then, when their speedboat arrived, Dodi took me aside and asked me to bring a fruit basket quickly. I hurriedly found one and brought it to him. Suddenly, to my great surprise, he starting throwing fruit at his uncle, who was already in the speedboat below. Salah laughed, picked up the fruit that was landing all around him and threw it back. Soon fruit was flying furiously back and forth between the *Jonikal* and Salah's speedboat, with Dodi and his uncle laughing like two small boys pitching water balloons at each other! Maybe it was a family tradition or maybe some sort of revenge for another fruit fight; I didn't know. But it was good natured, whatever the reason. Even the princess joined in, grabbing some grapes and tossing them at Uncle Salah. The fruit fight continued even as the speedboat pulled away, with Dodi, Diana and Salah laughing as if their sides would split.

Arms around each other, wiping tears of laughter from their eyes, the two lovers retreated to their favorite evening hideaway, the open-air salon. As they snuggled on the couch, they asked me to play *The English Patient* soundtrack again and bring them their customary mint tea. With lights dimmed and candles lit, they lay back on the couch holding hands, enjoying the richness of their growing love.

CHAPTER 7

Dodging the Paparazzi

Cruising off the coast of the Italian Riviera on a bright, windy afternoon a couple of days later, my boss made an unusual request.

"Rene, please have the crew put some canvas up to hide us as we eat lunch today."

I knew instantly why he wanted me to do this. The paparazzi had been on our trail during the entire trip, but now they were hovering in their boat right nearby, cameras trained directly into the *Jonikal*'s dining room. Can you imagine the indignity of it? Dodi and the princess couldn't even eat lunch on their own boat in the middle of the ocean without someone taking pictures of them!

Soon the crew had set up a large canvas screen that completely blocked the paparazzi's view of our dining table, and *our* view of everything else. The wind was really kicking up, so we had to keep an eye on the canvas, which threatened to blow away a couple of times; but at least the two lovers were able to enjoy their lunch in peace. Unfortunately, this incident was just a small indication of a growing problem.

The "paparazzi issue" had been bothering Dodi for some time. Although he and the princess had managed to evade them for most of the first trip, all bets were off now. During this voyage they dogged us mercilessly, never more than a few hundred yards away. Their huge telephoto lenses were constantly trained on our vessel, in the same way that a hunter lines up the crosshairs on his prey. The instant either Diana or Dodi appeared on deck, they snapped away and, as illustrated by the lunchtime episode, even tried to photograph them through the windows.

Until you have witnessed firsthand the invasiveness and aggressiveness of these acts, you can't really understand how disturbing it is psychologically. Your adrenaline starts racing whenever you see these people lurking around. It makes you want to run and hide or scream and shout at them, but there's nothing you can do to make them leave you alone permanently. This kind of treatment is nothing short of inhumane; there should be laws against such blatant harassment.

Once their canvas-shielded lunch had been completed, I could tell that Dodi, fed up with the paparazzi's tactics, was ready to take action. He asked Trevor and Luigi to take one of the speedboats over to the paparazzi's boat and ask them to please give us a little privacy. On that particular day, they were close enough so that I could hear the sounds of what became a heated discussion between Trevor, Luigi and the photographers. And I could certainly tell by everyone's body language that it was not a pleasant conversation.

When they returned, a frustrated, red-faced Trevor reported that the paparazzi were not in a cooperative mood. Dodi was unhappy, but what could he do? The ocean is public property, which meant that the paparazzi, unfortunately, had as much right to be there as we did. Dodi stalked off toward his cabin, fuming and muttering, "Unbelievable. Just unbelievable."

Luckily, the princess was not on deck to witness any of this. Dodi tried to keep his concerns away from her as much as possible, not wanting to spoil the happy, relaxed atmosphere we'd all worked so hard to create; but she could hardly help but be aware of the constant intrusion. Dodi began to spend more time making intricate plans with the security guards, to evade the paparazzi. At one point, he even asked me to pitch in and help shield the princess.

One day Debbie and I noticed that Diana was quite upset. Seeing that she was trying to hide her tears, we left her alone, retreating to the little kitchen. We were glad to see that Dodi was immediately by her side, comforting her and talking in a low, reassuring voice. It was painful to see the princess in such a state without knowing how to help her. We thought the best thing to do was just give them their privacy, while always being nearby, ready to fulfill any requests. This is actually trickier than it sounds—you want to be available and yet you want to leave them alone. Luckily, it wasn't long before she had regained her sunny disposition and started smiling again. But we had all been disturbed by her unhappiness, especially Dodi. I don't know what had bothered her so. It might be that the paparazzi had pushed too hard. She was used to dealing with them, of course, but she was only human. Like all of us, she had a breaking point.

Oblivious to the pain they caused by their endless stalking, the paparazzi hovered behind us, lenses trained on the *Jonikal*. We were all beginning to get really angry. But the following day we turned the tables on them. On this particular morning we got under way early, heading to Sardinia. Dodi came to the pilot house after breakfast and I waited nearby as he quietly conferred with Luigi. A few moments later, I heard Luigi laugh and say, "OK, OK."

Soon I noticed that the *Jonikal* was doing an about-face. In no time at all, we had turned one hundred and eighty degrees and were facing the paparazzi head on. We plowed straight ahead, right at them! Everyone came up on deck to watch, including the princess. When the paparazzi realized what was happening, they didn't know if we were just kidding or truly determined to ram them. Still, they weren't taking any chances. Turning tail, they sped off at top speed, anxiously looking back to see how serious we were.

When we made them run, all of us, including Diana, screamed, yelled and jumped for joy. Again, we had the upper hand with those vultures! We followed them until we were within about a hundred yards, just to give them a good scare, then turned around and resumed our original course. The princess was triumphant, jumping up and down like a schoolgirl. This little adventure lifted everybody's spirits for the entire day.

The next morning, just after breakfast, Dodi and Diana decided to go for a swim and do a little Jet-Skiing. We were approximately five hundred yards from one of the beaches in Sardinia. Although it was very quiet, there were some people around.

"Rene, go change," my boss instructed. "Wear your bathing suit and life jacket. I want you to use the Jet Ski to stay close to us."

I changed quickly and plunged into the ocean. The Jet Ski sat waiting for me in the water, gleaming in the sunlight. I looked at it for a moment, climbed up on the running board and got into position. Then I just sat there, puzzled. Finally, feeling very stupid, I said to a couple of crew members, "How do you start this thing?" I'd never been on a Jet Ski in my life! My job was to take care of my boss and his guests, which precluded Jet-Skiing about one hundred percent of the time. At least it did until that particular day.

The crew laughed at my confusion, then one of them said, "Rene, you drive a motorcycle. It starts the same way."

Somehow I managed to fire up the engine and shakily take off. In no time I was Jet-Skiing, semiconfidently, behind my boss and the princess. That was one thing about my job—I never knew what I'd be called upon to do next. At least it kept things interesting!

I quickly caught up with the two lovers, who were riding together on one Jet Ski, she behind him, her arms around his waist. At one point, they swooped way in toward the shore, coming within fifteen yards of the beach, where she jumped off and started to swim. Dodi blasted back toward me and shouted, "Rene, I'm going to take a little drive on the Jet Ski. Please stay close by her." Then he roared off.

Even though we had Trevor nearby in a small motorboat, I zipped around behind the princess from one side to the other in an arc, watching for anyone who might annoy her. A few people in small boats recognized her (or maybe they recognized the name *Jonikal*) and tried to get in close for a better look. But as they began to draw nearer, I'd zoom over to them and say "Please, stay back" as nicely as I could, hoping they would respond to a friendly request. Fortunately, everyone did, but it got wearing after a while. It seemed that every little thing the princess wanted to do turned into a big deal, through no fault of her own.

She swam for at least fifteen minutes while Dodi had a good time zipping up and down and around the *Jonikal*. Then, when the princess started to swim back to the boat, Dodi pulled up alongside her.

"Madame," he said gallantly, "could I offer you a ride?"

She laughed and replied, "No thank you, sir. My mother told me never to accept a ride from a stranger."

She ducked under the water, coming up again several feet away, where she began her strong, rhythmic stroke. But she called over to me, "Rene, please follow me back, in case I have trouble."

I fell into position parallel to her, watching carefully as she swam. This was the first time I had really looked closely at her style, which was impressive. Her strokes were strong and graceful. Once she finally reached the ladder that led to the main deck, she hung on to its railing, catching her breath and relaxing. I sat next to her on the Jet Ski and said, "Madame, you swim like a mermaid. If I ever have a problem while swimming, I hope you'll be watching over me."

She laughed with pleasure. "Yes," she said brightly. "Maybe someday I can return the favor."

One afternoon toward the end of our trip, I came upstairs to the sundeck, arriving just as Dodi was excusing himself to make a phone call.

I said, "Madame, is there anything you'd like, perhaps some cookies?"

"No, no thank you, Rene. Everything is wonderful."

I turned and began walking toward the stairs when she called me back, her voice soft but rather urgent. I was at her side immediately, a questioning look on my face.

"Rene," she began, rather hesitantly. "Was Dodi always this nice and gentle with other women?"

I had known my boss for more than seven years. A host of incidents flashed through my mind as I stopped to think. Then I knelt down so that I could talk to her quietly, face-to-face.

"Madame," I said softly, "I don't talk about Mr. Fayed's behavior, mood or anything else. But this time, I'm going to make an exception because people are talking a lot about Mr. Fayed now. We see things about him in the papers that are not very nice. But these people don't really know him. They may have just met him briefly at a meeting, or a party, or the opening night of a movie. Then there are old girlfriends who are coming out of the woodwork, but as we all know, an old lover often has an axe to grind.

"Yes, he was always kind and gentle to women in the past. But one thing, Madame, I swear to you: I have never seen Mr. Fayed as happy and as much in harmony with his surroundings as he has been since he met you."

She smiled, dropping her eyes for a moment before looking back at me.

"Thank you, Rene," she said softly. "I appreciate it."

I stood up, knowing it was time to leave her alone with her thoughts.

"I'll come back in a few minutes to check on you," I promised.

"Rene," she said, placing an urgent hand on my arm, "please don't say anything about this to Dodi."

"Madame," I replied, "what was said is just between you and me."

As I left, I had conflicting feelings. On the one hand I was glad to help ease any worries the princess might have had about Dodi, especially after reading what the newspapers were saying about him—that he was just a rich man's son, a playboy, a dilettante, a good-for-nothing. On the other hand, I felt uncomfortable speaking about my boss behind his back. But if I didn't tell the princess the truth about what a fine person he was, who would? I wanted her to know, and I knew that Dodi also wanted her to know, that he was absolutely sincere. In this one instance, I felt sure that he wouldn't mind my personal revelations about him.

That night we were to host another dinner party, but this time the guests would be Dodi's half-sister, Jasmine, a very beautiful sixteen-year-old girl whom I'd met in Gstaad a couple of years earlier, and one of her girlfriends. Jasmine was very excited that night, not because she was visiting the yacht, but because she would be seeing Diana again.

Dodi requested an early dinner, meaning we would begin to serve them around half past eight or nine, making it one of the earliest dinners of the trip.

The princess, Dodi and I waited for the girls on deck and greeted them there, just as we would "important" adult guests. I thought it was a very thoughtful and respectful thing for them to do. Dodi then escorted Diana and the girls to the outdoor salon to have drinks and a chat. The princess and Dodi already had their wine, so I brought the girls some orange juice. After a short period of time, perhaps fifteen or twenty minutes, Dodi signaled me, saying, "Rene, we are ready whenever you are." I began the dinner service.

During the meal, the princess gave her full attention to Jasmine and her friend, as I had come to expect of her. Again, she played the role of hostess beautifully, getting totally involved in what they were saying, never allowing her attention to wander. The conversation was animated, punctuated by lots of laughter, and Dodi teased Jasmine about soon being seventeen. Jasmine spoke about how badly she wanted a little Mercedes for her birthday. I think she was taking driving lessons. All in all, it was a delightful evening for everyone. I was struck by the way the princess always seemed to enjoy others, whether they were young or old, important or just average, everyday people.

When the girls finally said goodbye and sped off in their motorboat, Diana and Dodi leaned on the railing, watching them go.

"Oh, how refreshing this evening was," the princess said, smiling at Dodi with just a touch of sadness in her face. She had enjoyed herself immensely with the teenagers, perhaps because they reminded her of her own cherished sons.

A few days later, we had a bit of a scare. The *mistral*, a strong, cold, northerly wind from the south of France, had kicked up, and for two days it churned the sea and blew furiously across the *Jonikal*'s decks. I don't know how fast it was blowing, but it reminded me of riding my motorcycle at seventy miles an hour with no helmet! The *Jonikal* sailed close to land rather than out on the open seas for maximum protection from the *mistral*, and we stayed inside as much as possible, going out on deck only when absolutely necessary.

At about two in the afternoon, I went to check on

my boss, who was working on his computer in the indoor dining room. He looked up and asked if I'd seen the princess.

"I don't think she's outside, Mr. Fayed," I said, "but I'll check."

Bracing myself against the wind, I fought my way up and down the walkways on the first deck. Nothing. I ducked into the enclosed salon, scanning the room and again found nothing. Hmmm. Not in the main dining room or out by the speedboats on the second level, either. *She certainly wouldn't be up on the sundeck in all this wind*, I thought, but I forced myself to run up the steps for a quick check anyway. The helipad was bare, of course, and so was the area where the lounge chairs usually sat, since the crew had gathered them up and stowed them safely inside. A "tunnel" through an array of electronic equipment connected the lounge chair area to the front part of the sundeck, where the built-in couches were. Stepping into this tunnel, I took a quick look around the front part of the sundeck but saw no one. The bright yellow cushions and towels had all been collected, leaving nothing but the bare bones of the built-in couches that ran along the perimeter. She wasn't there, of course.

Concerned, I returned to my boss.

"Mr. Fayed," I reported, "I looked everywhere but I couldn't find her."

"My God!" he said, alarmed. "You don't think she could have blown overboard, do you?"

"Oh no, Mr. Fayed," I reassured him, although I

really wasn't at all convinced. "I'm sure she's somewhere in the boat. Let me find out if Debbie knows where she is."

"OK," he replied worriedly. "But keep it quiet. Let's not start a panic."

Debbie hadn't seen the princess either, so Dodi and I decided to make one more careful check before we really started to get frightened. After all, it was a big boat and there were many places that the princess could be. She usually stayed on the three "guest" levels, since she had no reason to go below into the crew, engine and work areas. But maybe, just maybe, she was wandering around someplace unusual. Dodi told me he would look inside, while I should look outside.

Once again the wind blasted me as I made my rounds, looking everywhere. Where in the world could she be?

By now I had begun to run up and down the stairs to the various levels, walking quickly on the walkways so as not to attract attention. Finally, heart pounding, I ran up the stairway to the sundeck, and once again stood under the electronics array. As before, the deck lay empty. Then, for some reason, I decided to walk all the way through the tunnel and go onto the sundeck proper. When I did, I immediately caught sight of her, sitting on the floor of the deck at the very edge of the cushionless couches, with her knees drawn up to her chest, protecting against the wind. She was talking on her cellular phone, apparently enjoying herself. She waved and gave me a little smile as she continued chatting. I breathed a huge sigh of relief and ran down the stairs to ease my boss's mind. A look of relief crossed his face as he said, "How can she be out there in this kind of weather?"

On Thursday evening, August 28, as I brought cocktails to Diana and Dodi, snuggled on the overstuffed living room couch, my boss said, "Here you go, Rene," handing me one of his expensive Cohiba Borrusto cigars. It was not the first time he'd done this; he'd generously given me some of these high-quality cigars before. They were so much better than the two-dollar cigars I normally smoked.

"Thank you," I replied, putting it in my vest pocket. "I'll save it for a special occasion."

"This is a special occasion, Rene," the princess piped up excitedly. "Today—August 28—is the anniversary of my divorce!"

"Madame," I replied, "if that is the case, I will be sure to smoke the cigar tonight in your honor."

She nodded approvingly, then beamed at Dodi as she reached for his hand. In a year's time she had seemingly made a very successful transition from divorced woman to woman in love. I could tell she was very happy about it.

It was still twilight, only about eight o'clock on a beautiful, calm evening. I was looking forward to our usual leisurely pace; dinner wouldn't be served for at least another two hours. Perhaps I'd even have time to try out my new cigar. But the next time I checked on them, Dodi greeted me with an excited look on his face.

"Rene, you know what?" he asked brightly.

My heart sank. What did he have in mind this time?

"The princess and I would like to have a barbecue."

Oh, is that all? I thought. That doesn't sound so bad. Then he let the axe fall.

"On the beach," he said.

A barbecue on the beach? Such things normally took hours to arrange!

"But Mr. Fayed," I protested, "it's already eight o'clock. We're not prepared to make a barbecue tonight!"

"It's OK," he answered reassuringly. "Take your time. We'll have a late dinner tonight. Go see Luigi. He'll take you to the beach so you can find an area where we can have a very nice evening."

Ah, lovers! There's no telling when they'll be in the mood for an amorous getaway. And what could be more conducive to love than a secluded beach and a roaring fire? I could see why they wanted to do it, but it was very difficult to pull off at the last minute. I knew I had my work cut out for me. Luigi said he'd take a crew member ashore and find a good spot so I could stay on the boat to prepare. He was as good as his word, and within half an hour, we could see a fire burning on the shore.

I hurried down to the galley to give Christiano the bad news. His eyes widened with disbelief as he immediately started pulling hamburgers, sausages, ribs and anything else he could think of out of the refrigerator. Debbie helped me gather plates, glasses, salt, pepper, napkins, six or seven little folding tables we normally used on the sundeck, a tablecloth, blankets and any other items we would need. We had to have it all because, once on the beach, there would be no quick trips back to the kitchen.

Luigi returned in the tender and with our hastily assembled load ready, Christiano, Trevor and I set off for shore. By the time we arrived on the beach, it was completely dark. The firelight was our only source of illumination. Christiano lit his barbecue, which took half an hour to become fully heated, while I looked around to find the best place to set up the table. About an hour and a half had elapsed since Dodi first said, "Rene, you know what?"

Soon, Trevor and Luigi and I were clearing an area not too far from the fire, smoothing the sand to make sure it was nice and flat and had no little rocks or sticks protruding. I laid a big blanket over the area, then set up the little tables. By putting two or three together, then covering them with a tablecloth, I was able to create an instant full-size table. Two other little tables placed next to this big table would serve as chairs. The experience of setting up a "dinner for two" in Ed McMahon's unfinished house was coming in handy!

Before long, I thought I had everything under pretty good control and was just putting the wine into an ice bucket when the wind abruptly shifted, sending a shower of sparks all over the picnic area. Moving fast, I had to pull the whole ensemble—tables, chairs, blankets—around to the other side of the fire, just in time to have the wind change and blow sparks all over *that* area! The wind continued playing games, forcing me to move everything three or four times before finally settling down.

Finally, the table was ready, just as the tender pulled ashore. I lit the candles, quickly reminded Christiano that Dodi liked his meat very well done, then went to greet the couple. As they hopped out of the boat and walked up to our delightful little setting, the princess exclaimed, "My God, Rene, is there anything that you *can't* do?" With that comment, all the trouble seemed worth it.

Their magical evening began with the pouring of the wine. But instead of sipping it at my little table, the two decided to take their glasses and do a little exploring. They couldn't go very far, perhaps only fifteen or twenty yards in any one direction because beyond that there was no light and it was very rocky. So they went as far away as they could, sipping their wine and seeking a moment of privacy. Trevor, Christiano and I left them alone, and for a few blissful minutes they could act like any other couple in love, walking hand in hand on the beach, looking at the moon and sharing lovers' secrets. It was so dark and secluded, we might as well have been on the moon.

After their stroll, they sat down at my little table and asked for some of the princess' favorite caviar; incredibly, they continued to talk endlessly. After about a half hour of sipping wine and eating caviar, Dodi told us to begin grilling the meat—very well done for him, medium for the princess. Within minutes, dinner was ready to be served, the meat grilled to perfection.

"Sir," I announced, "whenever you are ready, we are ready."

"Let's eat!" Diana said impulsively. We all smiled.

We served three entrees that night: Dodi's favorite chicken burgers, smoked sausages and baby back pork ribs, beginning with the burgers. As usual they ate slowly, in no rush at all. I sat by the fire and checked on them every ten minutes or so to see if they were finished, but they were really taking their time. Dodi finished his chicken burger but the princess only ate half of hers, probably because she knew there were other courses to come. They sipped a little wine over the course of the evening, with the princess, as usual, taking only half a glass at a time.

When they finally completed their leisurely dinner, we began to gather everything for the journey back to the *Jonikal*. But Dodi and Diana had decided to stay on to enjoy the last of the fire and spend a little more time by themselves (along with the ever-present Trevor, of course). So we packed everything into the tender, hopped aboard and began slowly pulling away from the beach, leaving them behind. Looking back, we could see the fire still burning brightly, its red-orange flames the only source of illumination on the entire pitch-black island. And silhouetted in the firelight were the two lovers, standing with their arms wrapped around each other as if they had waited all evening for these moments of privacy. (Trevor had discreetly stepped aside, into the shadows.) It was the most romantic sight I have ever seen.

Suddenly, Luigi burst into song, singing lustily, "*Volare, oh oh. Contare, oh, oh, oh, oh.*" The rest of us joined in, singing loudly. From the beach, Dodi and the princess looked after our receding boat and waved. We waved back, cheering them on in song. We continued to sing during the entire trip back to the *Jonikal*, the magic and the romance of the evening filling our hearts with gladness. The memory of that evening still makes me smile.

The following day, Friday, August 29, was our last full day on the yacht. We were anchored about three hundred yards offshore at Cala di Volpe. A wealthy, secluded resort in northeast Sardinia, it is a rich man's paradise because of the privacy it affords. Unfortunately, that famed privacy would not be enjoyed by Diana and Dodi when they took the tender to shore in the early afternoon. Paparazzi swarmed around them like bees, flashing away. The princess was really yearning for a swim, so she, Dodi and the bodyguards piled into the tender again and took off for one of the resort's private coves. There, shielded by the tender and the crew members, they were able to swim and splash around without being overly harassed. I watched them through binoculars as they clung to each other, heads bobbing above the blue-green water. At one point, laughing, she jumped into his arms like a bride being carried over the threshold and wrapped her arms around his neck. Even from my perspective, I could tell he loved it.

In the evening, they decided to take their chances by going ashore again for a little walk, this time inviting me to join them. We didn't leave for shore until approximately eleven o'clock and it was a little cold that night, so we all put on sweaters before getting into the tender. At the dock, as usual, Dodi, Diana, Kes, Trevor and I climbed out, leaving Luigi behind, and took up our typical formation: I walked in front, followed by the two lovers holding hands, with the ever-vigilant Trevor and Kes bringing up the rear.

We strolled in and around the Cala di Volpe Hotel and window-shopped at their little boutique before coming upon a beautiful, picturesque, dimly lit little garden. Wisteria trailed over an archway, bougainvillea overflowed with vibrant color and night-blooming jasmine scented the air. It was truly a little corner of paradise, right here in the middle of this small Sardinian village. Trevor, Kes and I stayed behind as Diana and Dodi took a ten-minute stroll through this enchanted place. Then we continued our walking and window-shopping.

At one point, Dodi saw something he wanted to buy, but he hadn't brought his wallet. He quietly told me to ask Trevor, who was standing some distance away, if he'd brought Dodi's wallet. Trevor's reply was "No, I don't have any money with me." Trevor then asked Kes if he had any money, but he didn't either. So we went back to the tender to see if Luigi had any. No luck.

The whole situation struck me as funny. Out of our little group of six, including one of the richest men in the world and the Princess of Wales, none of us had a dime (or a lira) in our pockets! I did have a credit card, which I gladly offered to my boss, the person who had always been so generous to me, saying, "Mr. Fayed, I have my credit card. If you need something, there is no problem."

"No, no, it's OK," he said, and we continued on. The moment had obviously passed, and whatever he had wanted to buy was no longer important.

We strolled around for half an hour, then returned to the hotel. There we heard music coming from a small cocktail lounge. We didn't go in; instead we simply stopped for a few moments to look and listen. After that, Dodi wanted to go back to the secret little garden for a few more moments. It was as if he didn't want to let the magic go—not just yet. So back we went.

Although nothing much had happened on our little promenade, Dodi looked as if he were walking on a cloud. He wore the smile of absolute contentment, something I had never seen before he met the princess. He had obviously discovered that the most wonderful and enjoyable things are the simplest ones, especially when you're in love. Just holding your lover's hand, walking down the street and being able to say, "Look at that! Isn't it great?" can bring a happiness and satisfaction unmatched anywhere else in the universe. This, I was certain, was what Dodi was feeling. My boss, who had spent his entire life helping himself to the finest offerings of the material world, finally had it all.

Holding hands, the two lovers spent a few more minutes alone in the enchanted little garden, walking around it very, very slowly, as if to breathe in its beauty and mystery, then lock it away in their hearts forever. When they were finally finished, we casually strolled back to the tender. It was after midnight when we got back to the *Jonikal*, and while the crew stowed the tender, Dodi and Diana retired to the circular couch in the open-air salon. As I served them mint tea, Dodi asked me to turn on the TV and VCR and to set out a few tapes that they could choose from.

Then I retreated to my favorite "private" area, on the walkway just outside the little kitchen, where I smoked one of the great Cohiba Borrusto cigars that Dodi had given me, sipped a little juice and thought about my future with Dodi and the princess in Malibu. I could hardly believe it but, after three years in Europe, I was finally going home to Los Angeles, where I'd be working for people who treated me almost like one of the family. I also thought about how privileged I had been to witness the birth of this beautiful love affair, one I was sure would last forever. I would always feel close to them because of that.

I checked on them one more time and Dodi waved me off. They were curled up together on the couch; the VCR and the TV had not been touched.

"Thank you, Rene," he said. "We won't be needing anything else."

As I turned to leave, I heard the princess call softly, "Thank you, Rene."

I turned back and she smiled at me, her eyes soft and glowing with love.

"Sleep well," she said.

"Thank you, Madame," I replied. "I wish you the same."

Who could have imagined that they had less than twenty-four hours to live?

CHAPTER

8

An End to Love

Saturday morning, August 30, dawned clear, warm and serene off of Sardinia's Emerald Coast, where the securely anchored *Jonikal* bobbed easily in the azure waters. All of us were a little sad and subdued that morning because no one wanted to see our adventure come to an end. We were all returning to our "real lives," for better or for worse.

"You know, Rene," the princess said thoughtfully over her breakfast of orange juice and fresh fruit, "I've had such a wonderful time, I really hate to leave, especially since I know I'm going to be hounded by the paparazzi even more than I usually am."

I nodded sympathetically. "Yes, Madame. It really is a shame that they can't give you some breathing room once in a while."

"But," she said, her face brightening, "I get to see my boys tomorrow! I've missed them so much! I haven't seen them in a whole month and they're due to start school next week, so I have to grab whatever time I can get."

The boys, who had been vacationing with their father in Scotland, were obviously the light of her life.

"I'm sure they've missed you too, Madame," I said sincerely. "I hope you and your sons will have a fantastic time together. I know from experience that they grow up so quickly."

She nodded wistfully.

After breakfast, I turned my attention to the last-minute details. The night before, I had carefully packed most of Dodi's things—his jeans, T-shirts, shorts and light cotton jackets—leaving out only the black shirt, vest and dark jeans that he would wear home, plus a few personal items. I'd also packed my own things, so all I had to do that morning was throw a few remaining items into our suitcases and lug them out to the deck. There I helped the crew begin to pile the luggage into the tender, but we would have to make two or three trips back and forth to shore before all of the gear and all of the people were finally on land.

The end of any trip is always depressing. It seems there are endless dreary cleanup and hauling chores to do, with nothing much to look forward to at the other end. I hopped into the tender with the first load of luggage to make the trek to shore, ending up at the same small hotel, the Cala di Volpe, that we'd visited the night before. We unloaded the luggage and I stayed with it on the dock while the tender went back and forth, ferrying people and the rest of the luggage. Standing there with the hot Mediterranean sun beating down on my shoulders, I thought to myself that this was going to be a very long day. My boss and Diana would be returning to Paris that night, along with me, which meant that I'd be up at least until one in the morning. Who could have foreseen that it would end up being the longest day of my life?

It took three taxis to handle the lot of us. I squeezed into one with Myraiah and a big load of luggage. Kes and Debbie, with even more luggage, got into another, while Dodi, Diana and Trevor took a third. The princess had changed out of her usual shorts-and-a-top attire and looked wonderfully bronzed and relaxed in a casually chic tan pants suit with a black top. My boss, darkly handsome in the black shirt, vest and jeans that I'd laid out for him, was a fitting consort for her.

As we wound along the twisted roads of the rugged Sardinian coastline, I fell into a subdued and introspective mood. I knew that the easygoing rhythm we'd established on the boat would now be cast aside, as we substituted the harsher, higher-energy rhythms of the big city. I also knew, just from what I'd already witnessed, that the paparazzi were going to become an even bigger problem once we got home. After all, we'd be much more accessible to them. But I took solace in the fact that before long—maybe in just another month—we'd be moving to Los Angeles. There, I hoped we would all be able to recapture at least some of the peace and happiness that we'd enjoyed on the boat.

Myraiah and I were the first to arrive at Sardinia's

Olbia airport. We were also the first to board the sleek, powerful Gulfstream IV jet. Decorated in rose, pale aqua and tan, with Egyptian motifs on the fabric-covered walls and plenty of brown marble trim, the Gulfstream IV was the last word in deluxe air travel. The passenger area was divided into two parts: the front half had several extra-wide, superluxurious armchairs plus four couchlike seats and a couple of marble end tables. Each armchair was situated next to a large oval window and had more leg room that any basketball player would need. The front two chairs were placed face-to-face, the way they might be in a train compartment, so two people could carry on a conversation. The back half of the plane had smaller seats, but they were almost as luxurious as those in front.

As Myraiah and I waited for the others, we took pictures of each other inside the plane, laughing and goofing around a little. Then, glancing out the window, I saw the others arrive. As they pulled up, I could see that the paparazzi had seemingly sprung out of nowhere and were taking pictures from a short distance away. Well aware of this, Dodi and Diana rushed from the taxi into the plane.

Trevor, Debbie, Kes and Myraiah respectfully moved to the back of the aircraft as Dodi and the princess boarded. I started to follow them.

"Rene," my boss called after me. "Stay up here with us."

Great! I thought. *I get to sit in one of the deluxe seats!*

The lovers settled into the two plush chairs in front, facing each other, and according to my boss's instructions I sat in the chair right behind the princess. It had taken us longer than we'd planned to load the luggage and get everybody settled, so we ended up sitting on the runway for about thirty minutes, waiting for a new take-off time. Finally, at about half past one, we blasted down the runway and lifted off into heavenly blue skies.

The Gulfstream IV had its own flight attendant, who came around to serve us refreshments as soon as we were safely airborne. Later on, she also brought a selection of magazines. I picked one that was unfamiliar to me at the time. As soon as I started flipping through it, though, I realized it was a British tabloid, the kind that spends big money acquiring articles and pictures that show how the rich and famous live. As I idly turned the pages, I came upon an article about my boss, which didn't surprise me. The combination of his wealth and his relationship with Diana made him perfect fodder for publications like this.

While I was reading, Dodi went to the cockpit to visit the captain, a standard practice for him. Just then the princess turned around in her chair and smiled at me. I smiled back, trying as subtly as I could to cover up what I was reading. Too late—she saw it.

"I saw that article," she said, grimacing. "Isn't it just horrible what they're saying about us?"

The gist of the article was that Dodi was with Diana only because she was famous and made him look good.

"Madame," I replied, searching for the right words, "as you know, bad news and scandal sell magazines and newspapers. If they don't have something nasty to say, they make it up. But whatever they say about you and

Mr. Fayed won't matter to the people who know you and love you. None of the nonsense they print will tarnish you in their eyes."

She smiled gratefully. "Thank you very much, Rene. You're very sweet." She sighed, then brightened. "Oh, Rene," she said happily, "I'm so excited to see my two boys!"

After Dodi returned, they talked, laughed, glanced through magazines and sipped mineral water. It wasn't long before we were at Le Bourget airport, about ten miles north of Paris, touching down gently before roaring to a stop. Unfortunately, we had a welcoming committee of about ten paparazzi waiting for us.

From the window, I could see two cars waiting—a black Mercedes and my boss' black Range Rover. We had all seen the paparazzi, so we moved quickly. We wanted to get out of the plane and into the cars as fast as possible. Trevor was the first one out of the jet, followed closely by Diana, then Kes, Dodi and me. My boss stopped to talk to a heavy-set, balding man in a gray suit and dark glasses. Although I'd never seen this man before, I would soon know his name well. It was Henri Paul.

Minutes later, Dodi, the princess and Trevor drove off in the Mercedes, with Philippe at the wheel. Debbie, Myraiah, Kes and I followed in the Range Rover, driven by Henri Paul. We had a police escort until we hit the A1 autoroute, but no farther. Unfortunately, that was the exact spot where the paparazzi caught up with us.

Although we were clipping along at a pretty good

speed, a couple of cars and some motorcycles stayed right behind us, making calls on their cellular phones as they flew down the road. Then a black car sped ahead of us and ducked in front of the Mercedes, braking and making us slow down so the paparazzi on motorcycles could get more pictures. It was really frightening to see how aggressively these people could behave, all in the name of getting what would probably be a pretty lousy picture! They were risking their lives and ours, just to get a shot of Dodi and Diana riding in a car. Unbelievable!

At some point along the way, our caravan split up. Although I thought we were going to the apartment, Henri was suddenly heading in a different direction.

"Where are we going?" I asked, puzzled.

"I'm trying to make the paparazzi follow me," he said. "I'm hoping they'll leave the Mercedes alone while they go off on an errand." He zipped down the road while executing a few evasive actions designed to make it look as though Diana and Dodi were riding in our car. Kes didn't appear concerned, so I figured it was all part of a plan. And looking out the back window, I saw that it seemed to work. Two small paparazzi cars were on our tail.

Later I would learn that Dodi had taken Diana to the Bois de Boulogne to see Windsor Villa, the place where I took the dogs for their daily run. By all accounts, Dodi hoped to make it a home for the two of them whenever they were in Paris.

After the long, harrowing ride, I was relieved when we finally arrived at the apartment around four-thirty.

Henri Paul dropped us off, helped unload our luggage and drove down the Champs-Elysées. After helping Debbie and Myraiah get settled in their room on the fourth floor, I was at last able to let myself into Dodi's second-floor apartment. Lugging my gear into the foyer, I thought I had never been so happy to see its pink, black and white marble floors and elegant golden chandelier. Home sweet home! All I wanted was a shower, a change of clothes and a moment to put my feet up.

But first I had to deal with the boxes waiting for me in the foyer. I'd called the Ritz that morning from the yacht to order flowers, caviar and other needed items, knowing it would be too late if I waited until I got home. I quickly stowed the caviar and other perishables in the refrigerator, then found some crystal vases, filled them with water and put out the flowers. Catching sight of the clock I realized, unhappily, that it was already nearly five. I needed to start preparing for the evening's activities and I still wasn't sure exactly what was going on. I had to be ready for anything.

I hustled my bags down the hall to my room, but just as I set them down, the phone rang. It was Dodi.

"Rene," he said, "we are at the hotel. We'll be at the apartment in about an hour and a half, so have some appetizers ready."

I hurriedly unpacked and took a shower, dressing once again in my uniform. I washed and dried some crystal wineglasses, made sure the wine was cooling in the refrigerator, arranged the appetizers and made a quick check of the apartment. At last, all was ready for them. Although a little tired from the trip, I was still looking forward to the evening and to serving the princess once again.

At about seven, although everything had been prepared, checked and rechecked, my boss and the princess still hadn't arrived. Glancing out the window to the rue Arsene-Houssaye, where the front door of our building was situated, I was startled to see a band of paparazzi waiting for them. Obviously, they knew Diana and Dodi were in Paris and would eventually come to the apartment.

Oh no, I thought. *I hope they aren't going to spoil the evening.*

Just then I saw the black Mercedes and the Range Rover pull up. Although I was silently cheering for my boss and the princess, hoping the paparazzi wouldn't bother them too much, I could see they were being mobbed. I heard the shouting, saw flashes going off and watched a security guard shove one of the photographers. Dodi did his best to shield Diana as Trevor and Kes fought to clear a path to the door, allowing the lovers to run into the building. More than a little shaken by what I had just seen, I prepared to greet them at the door.

The princess was ashen and trembling, and Dodi was angry as they stalked through the apartment door with Kes and Trevor on their heels.

"Go out there and tell them to back off!" Dodi instructed the bodyguards. "This is absurd!"

Kes and Trevor went back down to talk to the paparazzi, while I brought the luggage inside and served the couple some Evian water to help them calm down. While they recuperated, I put Dodi's luggage in his suite and the princess' in the green salon that was just off the marble foyer.

After a short time, good humor somewhat restored, Dodi and Diana began to prepare for one last night on the town before her return to London. Diana had already had her hair done at the Ritz and now just wanted to bathe, change and redo her makeup. In the guest bathroom next to the green salon, she unpacked her toiletries and set out small jars of Estée Lauder cream, bottles of Chanel perfume, makeup and other items. She then took a long bath. Dodi, in the meantime, went to shower in the master bathroom—a room so huge that it contained a king-sized Jacuzzi, an extra-large shower, a sauna and even a bed to rest on afterward!

I had laid out the clothes that Dodi wanted to wear that evening—blue jeans, a light gray shirt, a brown suede jacket and cowboy boots. Then, since I was already prepared for the cocktail hour, I retired to my quarters and waited.

Worn out from the day's activities, I sat in my easy chair, listening for the slight rattling of my door that would tell me someone was entering the kitchen. I soon heard it and I was automatically on my feet and in motion. I met Dodi as he walked through the kitchen doorway, his eyes gleaming with excitement.

It was then that he showed me the ring.

"Make sure we have champagne on ice when we come back from dinner," he told me urgently. "I'm going to propose to her tonight!"

I nodded, feeling almost as excited as if I were the one making the marriage proposal. Every bit of my fatigue had vanished; I felt like dancing on the rooftops!

Several minutes later I came across the princess standing in the foyer, dressed for dinner in a black top with matching jacket, white pants and black high-heeled sling-back pumps. She looked lovely—freshly coiffed and made up, relaxed, tanned and glowing from the trip.

When she saw me, she said, "Rene, do you have a brush?"

"A hairbrush?" I asked.

"No, a clothes brush," she replied. "I need to take some lint off of this jacket."

"Yes, Madame. I'll get you mine." Hurrying back to my quarters, I dug out my clothes brush and brought it to her.

"Would you like me to do it for you, Madame?" I asked.

"No, no, Rene, thank you. I will do it." She took the brush and went into the green living room.

Just then Dodi appeared and said, "Rene, would you put some music on? Julio Iglesias, please." As I fiddled with the CD player in the living room, the princess emerged wearing her newly brushed jacket and asking for her customary half glass of wine. Dodi sipped a little bit of vodka and the two of them sat listening to the music, perhaps a bit fatigued from the long day but smiling at each other and talking softly.

Ten minutes later, I brought caviar. They were now very close to each other on Dodi's favorite couch, holding hands, her head resting on his shoulder. It was a warm night, about seventy-seven degrees, and it somehow seemed to get warmer and warmer as the minutes ticked by. I was very excited because I knew he was about to propose. Suspense seemed to hang in the air—when was he going to do it? Would he propose to her right here in the living room before dinner? Or later, in the restaurant? Or perhaps he would wait until they came back for the champagne? I had seen Dodi put the ring in his pocket when we were in the kitchen, so it was possible he might pop the question at any time. In spite of my excitement, as I continued to serve them and check on them that evening, I tried to be as unobtrusive as possible. I certainly didn't want to walk in on the big moment.

When they had almost finished the caviar, I asked if they wanted a little more.

"No, Rene," the princess said. "I love caviar, but I had so much during the trip."

Dodi stood up, excused himself and went to his bedroom. The princess, warm and congenial as always, asked, "Rene, did you have a good time on the trip?"

"Madame, I had a tremendous time. I hope we do it again."

She smiled and said, "Oh, we'll do it again. We definitely will."

At about twenty past nine, I went back to the living room for my last check on them before they left for dinner. Their reservation was for nine forty-five at Chez Benoit, a trendy, very chic restaurant near the

The magnificent *Jonikal*, where much of Diana and Dodi's love affair took place. (*Sunday Mirror*)

Dressed in my "night uniform" aboard the Fayed yacht.

Dodi looking handsome and rugged in his polo outfit. (Rex Features)

This picture of Diana was taken right after the first trip aboard the *Jonikal*, when her love for Dodi had just begun to bloom. (Popperfoto)

Tired of being harassed by the paparazzi on our second *Jonikal* trip, Dodi ordered Captain Luigi to turn around and chase their boat away. You can see, on the right, our curved wake as we made a 180-degree turn.

Here I am sitting in the outdoor salon where I served dinner to Dodi and the princess almost every night on both cruises.

The *Jonikal*'s colorful living room, equipped with every creature comfort.

The Imperial Suite at the Ritz where Diana and Dodi had their last meal. (*Sunday Mirror*)

Tokens of love: the ring with which Dodi intended to propose to Diana, and a pair of handsome cufflinks she had given him. (*Sunday Mirror*)

The wineglass bearing Diana's lipstick imprint and fingerprints. She had sipped from this glass just before leaving the apartment on the night of the accident. Several days after the tragedy, while sitting despondently on the living room couch, I noticed the glass hidden among the crystal decanters on the coffee table. (*Sunday Mirror*)

Georges Pompidou center. As usual, I coughed to warn them that I was about to enter. As I stepped into the living room, I found them sitting on the couch facing each other, Dodi holding both her hands in his. They were looking deeply into each other's eyes and having what appeared to be a serious talk. I immediately stopped and backed away quietly. I wondered if this might be the moment of truth!

A few minutes later they were in the foyer, preparing to leave for the restaurant. I raised my eyebrows at Dodi, as if to ask, "Did you propose yet?" He just smiled at me and shook his head very slightly.

I opened the door for them and as they exited, Dodi said, "Rene, we'll see you later on tonight."

"Yes, sir," I replied. "Have fun tonight."

The princess gave me a little wave, calling, "Have a good night!" And with that, they were off.

As soon as they were gone, I went back to the living room to clean up, plumping the cushions and setting them back in place, and otherwise making sure the room was presentable. Then I went back through the kitchen to my quarters, where I ate my own dinner while watching television. It was nice and quiet, with no phone calls to disturb me, but I couldn't focus on what I was watching because I kept wondering how their evening was going. Was everything all right? There was no doubt that the food would be of the highest quality and perfectly cooked. The atmosphere would be elegant. But when would he ask her? And was she expecting a proposal tonight? I couldn't wait to hear the details.

Around midnight it occurred to me that I hadn't taken the dogs out for their customary run before bedtime. I wondered if I would have enough time before Dodi and Diana returned; it would take me only about ten minutes. I knew Philippe would be chauffeuring them, so I called him on his portable phone to find out the schedule.

"Hey, Philippe," I said when he answered. "I just want to know if I have time to take the dogs for a walk before they arrive."

Philippe paused for a second and then said, in a surprised tone, "They're not there yet?"

I thought he was kidding. "Well, you should know; they are with you."

"No, Rene," he said, sounding just a bit alarmed. "I was driving the Range Rover; they went in the other car. They should be there by now. Let me find out what's happening. I'll call you right back."

Well, they probably took the long route home, I thought. Unconcerned, I waited for his return call, listening all the while for the front door. Although I was unaware of it at the time, Diana and Dodi had aborted their plan to dine at Chez Benoit due to the mob of paparazzi outside. Instead, they had gone to the Ritz and dined alone in the Imperial Suite. Around midnight, when the couple was ready to come back to the apartment, Philippe, Kes and another chauffeur, Jean-François Musa, were instructed to create a diversion by driving off from the front of the Ritz in two decoy cars. Dodi, Diana and Trevor left from the back of the hotel, driven by Henri Paul.

A couple of minutes after his phone call to me, Philippe and the others pulled up outside the apartment. The Mercedes carrying Dodi and the princess was nowhere in sight. A band of paparazzi was still camped out there. When one of them received a call on his cellular phone and turned white as a sheet, Philippe and Musa insisted that he tell them what he'd heard. The news was absolutely devastating—Diana and Dodi had been involved in a terrible accident under the Alma Bridge. Philippe knew instantly that it had to be the accident he'd just driven past. He called me immediately, his voice ringing with urgency, fear and disbelief. I had no idea he was just outside the apartment house.

"Rene," he gasped, "there's been an accident. We think Dodi's car is involved."

I felt as if I'd been hit with a sledgehammer.

"My God!" I said. "How bad is it?"

"I don't know. I'm going to go now. I know where it happened and I'm going to go over there to see. I'll call you right back."

Unbeknownst to me, Philippe, Kes and Musa had come upon the scene of the accident just before I phoned them, although they hadn't realized that Dodi and the princess were involved. Because they had departed from the front of the Ritz as a decoy, while Dodi and Diana had departed from the back, they weren't following them. But by chance they happened to take the same route, coming up to the Alma Tunnel just after the accident had occurred. When people came rushing out of the tunnel to wave the traffic away, Philippe had simply taken a detour; moments later he received my call. When they arrived at the apartment and heard about the accident, Philippe realized with horror that it must have been the scene he'd just avoided. He and Musa dropped Kes off at the apartment to start making phone calls, and then raced back to the tunnel.

Meanwhile, up in the apartment, I sat on the edge of my chair, heart pounding, as I thought, *Dear God. Please don't let anything happen to them!* Suddenly the night seemed unbearably hot. There was nothing to do but sit and wait or pace the floor; I certainly couldn't concentrate on television or reading. I could only wonder—what's going on?

After another fifteen or twenty minutes of this hellish waiting, the phone rang again. I grabbed it instantly.

"Yes?" I barked.

"Rene," croaked Philippe in a strangled, tear-laden voice that warned me something horrific had happened. "Rene, I think Dodi is dead! He's gone!"

"What?!" I screamed.

"The accident was horrible," he stammered, barely able to get the words out. "The car is totally smashed."

"It cannot be," I insisted. My mind simply refused to believe that such a thing was possible. I was sure that any moment Dodi and the princess would walk in and say it had all been a mistake.

"I think he's dead," Philippe said, crying.

"What about the princess and the others?" I asked fearfully, almost not wanting to hear.

"I think the princess is still alive, but Dodi, Trevor

and Henri Paul are all dead. My God, Rene, I'm holding his hand right now but the doctor who was trying to revive him just told me that he died."

I had no words. I felt as if I were…nowhere. My body was not there. I hung up the phone and sat down in my favorite chair. I stayed there for at least ten minutes without moving, staring at the wall, numb. I simply couldn't take it in; I'd moved into another dimension. It was such an unbelievable shock. He was just here! How could he possibly be gone? As my mind began to realize the enormity of what had just happened, I was hit by a tidal wave of emotion. I broke down, sobbing as if my heart would break. Within the blink of an eye, Fate had demolished both a life and a beautiful love affair. How in the world could it end like this?

My first instinct was to pet the dogs, as if I were telling them that their master was gone. Then I switched on the Channel Two news, where they were already talking about the tragedy. They didn't have any pictures yet, nor did they mention any deaths; they just reported that there was a bad accident involving Princess Diana. I was hoping against hope that somehow Philippe had gotten it wrong, that the doctor had made a mistake and Dodi was really still alive, or the person who had died was actually someone else. I was grasping at straws.

I started to get calls from the other security guards and went down to the building manager's office, where Kes was phoning his superiors in London. They were trying to decide if they should inform Mr. Al Fayed immediately of his son's death or simply tell him there had been an accident, waiting until the death was officially confirmed. After a lot of discussion, they finally opted for the latter. I also made calls to each of my sons. We were in the building manager's office downstairs for a good half hour, but it was not very comfortable, so I suggested we continue making calls from the little office I had in my quarters. Kes agreed.

Back in the apartment, I switched on the TV just in time to hear the newscaster confirm what we were hoping against hope was not true: "There has been a car accident in the Alma Tunnel involving the Princess of Wales and her escort, Dodi Fayed. Fayed has died; Henri Paul, the driver, has also died. Bodyguard Trevor Rees-Jones is in bad condition, and the princess is suffering from a leg injury."

I sat down heavily, a leaden weight in my heart. Thinking of the beautiful love affair I had witnessed, I said to myself, "Oh God, please let at least one of them survive. My God, let her live, let her live! Don't let both of them be swept away!" I began to shake uncontrollably.

Kes was on the phone to London again to let them know that the news was official. Mr. Al Fayed, who was at his Oxted home that night, was informed and we heard that he would immediately board his helicopter and head for Paris.

For the next three or four hours I stayed glued to the television, waiting for some news—any news—about the state of the princess. There were no dramatic reports, in fact no real word on what was happening to her until, at around three-thirty or four in the morning, the anchor said, "We've just learned that Princess Diana, the Princess of Wales, has died." It was as if a knife had been plunged into my heart. Again, I cried like a baby. I just couldn't believe they were both gone.

I would find out later, as did the rest of the world, that a combination of factors contributed to this devastating accident—but the one that stood out in my mind, because I had witnessed it so often during the preceding weeks, was the aggressive, overly ambitious actions of the paparazzi. Not only did they chase the lovers' car until it crashed headlong into a concrete pillar, they leaped out of their vehicles to take pictures of the dead and dying as they lay helpless in the mangled car. I was so sickened when I read about this behavior, I had to put the paper down.

CHAPTER

9

Picking Up the Pieces

As the first pale streaks of dawn began to light up the Parisian sky, I stared out over the Champs-Elysées, bleary-eyed and exhausted. Kes and I had been up all night answering phone calls, watching the news, letting people in and out of the apartment and waiting for someone to tell us what to do next. I was still wearing my uniform, the clothes I was meant to be wearing as the lovers celebrated their impending marriage with a champagne toast. It seemed like a hundred years ago now.

Then, for the umpteenth time, the phone rang. I picked it up wearily. This time it was Claude Roulet, the assistant to the president of the Ritz.

"Rene," he said, "Mr. Al Fayed wants to spend a couple of hours in the Villa but nobody is there to take care of him. Could you go and serve him breakfast?"

I knew he meant Windsor Villa, the place that Dodi

and Diana had visited just the day before. I immediately answered, "But of course."

"Good," said Roulet. "I'll send Philippe to the Ritz to get food, then he'll take you to the Villa."

Incredible as it may seem, I had never met Mr. Al Fayed, although I had worked for his son for more than seven years. Naturally, I wanted to help him in his hour of grief, but at the same time I dreaded going. What could I possibly say to this poor man who had just lost his son? What words could comfort him? I had no idea how to act or what to do, but I knew I had to do my best, if only for Dodi's sake.

Philippe picked up two boxes of fruit, juice, croissants, Danishes and other items from the Ritz, then came to the apartment to get me. We drove to the Villa in silence, for there were no words to express the way we were feeling.

As we entered the grounds of Windsor Villa, I realized that this would be the first time I had ever been inside the house. During all my many visits to its grounds, I had never once gone inside or even looked in the windows. Now, as I walked through the elegant house, furnished with an exquisite mixture of eighteenth-century English furniture, original French pieces, royal banners and marbled walls, I was temporarily jolted from my misery by the sheer grandeur of it all. Mr. Al Fayed had certainly spared no expense when he refurbished this historic old home.

The housekeeper greeted us at the door and showed us where to put the boxes. I asked where Mr. Al Fayed liked to have his breakfast, then rapidly prepared the table, including an arrangement of fresh flowers, to make it as attractive as possible.

"What time did Mr. Al Fayed want his wake-up call?" I asked.

"He said around eight-thirty, which is right about now," she replied, picking up the phone.

Soon, Mr. Al Fayed emerged from his room, grief-stricken, drawn and pale but immaculately dressed. He came into the dining room and saw me, a stranger, waiting to serve him. "Mr. Al Fayed," I said, "I'm Rene. I'm very sorry to meet you under these circumstances, sir." He could only sigh deeply by way of reply.

"Just wait for me by the door," he said. Standing by the table, he drank a little orange juice and ate a little fruit and a few grapes. Then he asked me in a voice weakened with sorrow, "Why wasn't Philippe driving my son last night?"

I felt so sorry for him, but I had no answer. "I have no idea," I told him truthfully.

He sighed again. "Rene, go to the apartment. I will meet you there in a couple hours."

Philippe stayed behind to chauffeur Mr. Al Fayed, while I drove the Range Rover back to the apartment to wait for him. At about eleven, I got a call from security downstairs announcing that Mr. Al Fayed was on his way up. I immediately went to open the door, and stood there waiting for him to emerge from the elevator.

"Hello, Rene," he said softly. "Can you tell me where the luggage belonging to my son and the princess was put?"

"Mr. Al Fayed, Mr. Dodi Fayed's luggage is in his bedroom," I replied. "The bags belonging to the princess are in the green living room."

He nodded, then said, "Rene, please stay here." He obviously wanted his privacy as he made his way down the hall to his son's bedroom. But once there, he took less than two minutes to decide what he wanted to take away. Then he called me in and asked me to carry Dodi's luggage and some other items to the front door.

That task completed, we went to the green living room, where I showed him Diana's luggage. It was a matched set, with two larger bags and one small one.

"Was that all she had?" he asked.

"Yes, sir, she had the three pieces that you see." There were also a few other items that she had left out—the cosmetics she'd unpacked in the guest bathroom, her book, *On Being Jewish,* and some clothes draped over the sofa.

Mr. Al Fayed glanced over these few belongings before saying, "Rene, would you and Debbie help me put these things back in the bag?"

We opened her large suitcase and carefully put her clothes, book and a few other items inside. Mr. Al Fayed treated each item with great respect and reverence, in much the same way he had treated the princess when she was alive. At one point, he picked up the clothes brush that I had loaned her the previous night. As he carefully placed it into her bag I was about to say, "Sir, this is mine," but I could not. I didn't want him to think I was trying to take away a "souvenir" of the tragedy. Instead, I let it go.

Finally, when everything had been gathered up and handed to the security guard to be taken downstairs, Mr. Al Fayed turned to me.

"Rene," he said, looking into my eyes, "I know you took good care of my son, and I will take care of you."

I was touched that this man who had just suffered such a terrible loss would think of me and my welfare.

"Would you please stay here for a little while until I call you from London?" he asked.

"Of course," I answered.

"Where are the dogs?" he asked. "Can I see them?"

I opened the door to the hallway that separated the guest area from the main apartment, and Shoe and Romeo immediately bounded out, going directly to Mr. Al Fayed. He knelt down to pet them as Romeo tried to lick his face. Looking up at me, he asked, "Do you think they know that something has happened?"

I nodded vigorously. "I think they know something. They haven't slept since the accident; they've seen people coming and going. I'm sure they can tell we're upset. They know something has happened."

He petted them again and stood up. Then, just as he started to leave, he turned back, reaching into his pocket. With typical Fayed generosity and concern, he pulled out a wad of bills and handed them to me.

"Oh no, Mr. Fayed, I don't need that. I have everything I need," I protested.

He put the money into my hand insistently, saying, "It's OK, it's OK."

I didn't want to argue with him, so I took the

money and murmured, "Thank you very much, sir." Then he was gone.

Later, back in my room, I looked at the money he had given me. It was five thousand francs, about one thousand dollars.

Throughout the next several days I stayed in the apartment, looking after the dogs and receiving condolence phone calls. It was about all I could cope with; I was completely exhausted and had no will to do anything but stare at the wall. All I could think of was the loss of two people who were very dear to me.

Finally, concluding that it was time to face reality again, I shook myself out of my stupor. I decided to go through the apartment to make sure everything was in order in case Mr. Al Fayed came back.

I started with Dodi's expansive closets. The three sets of mirrored double doors covered an entire wall in his bedroom and I was very familiar with their contents. Everything was neatly hung or folded and stowed in its proper place; the sport shirts, dress shirts, jackets, fifteen black Armani suits, shoes and cowboy boots. As I glanced over the sumptuous contents of the closet, everything seemed in order. But suddenly, something out of place caught my eye. It was some sort of box—just a little one—perched on the closet shelf in plain sight, although I hadn't noticed it there before. Drawing closer, I caught my breath as I realized that it was the ring box, the one Dodi had so proudly opened in the kitchen to show me the diamond ring he planned to give Diana!

Trembling, I reached up and grasped the box,

bringing it down and cradling it in my hands. With my heart pounding, I slowly lifted the lid. There it was, the magnificent, diamond-encrusted ring. Evidently he had decided to wait until they returned from their special dinner before he proposed. He had undoubtedly planned to give her the ring and then call for champagne to celebrate. I was sick at heart, knowing how horribly awry his plans had gone. Who could ever have envisioned it?

I immediately contacted Mr. Al Fayed in London, telling the secretary at his office that I had to speak to him about an urgent matter immediately. Within minutes, my phone call was returned.

"Mr. Al Fayed," I said, my heart racing, "I have found a beautiful diamond ring."

He paused for a moment before replying.

"Did you find any other valuable items?"

"No, sir," I answered, "I haven't searched."

"Rene," he said, "why don't you look everywhere throughout the apartment, see if you can find any valuables belonging to my son. And make an inventory. In the meantime, call the Ritz. Tell them to send you a car. Then take the ring, in person, to Frank Klein at the hotel. And call me back."

The chauffeur came quickly and I was hustled off to the Ritz, carrying my precious cargo. I was escorted immediately to the office of Frank Klein, president of the Ritz. He and Claude Roulet were waiting for me. As soon as the door closed behind us, I produced the little box, which Mr. Klein carefully opened. I heard Claude Roulet murmur softly, "Yes, that's the ring, that's the one."

During a later conversation, Mr. Al Fayed asked me if I had found any other valuable items, particularly a set of cufflinks the princess had given Dodi. I continued my search but found nothing. The next day I looked again. I went back to Dodi's closet several times and stared at the clothes hanging neatly in place. Then, for some reason, I put my hands together and inserted them into the middle of the dozen pairs of hanging jeans, pushing them to either side. Below them, on a built-in wooden dresser, I discovered a brown briefcase that, by chance, was exactly the same color as the dresser. Because it blended in so well and was hidden by the hanging jeans, the briefcase had been perfectly camouflaged. Trying the latches, I discovered it was locked. Convinced that it contained something valuable, I immediately put another call through to Mr. Al Fayed.

The first thing he asked was, "Do you know the combination to the lock?"

"Sir, I do not, but the combinations for his suitcases were always zero-zero-zero."

"Try it," he replied.

I put the phone down, twirled the little number dials to zero-zero-zero and pushed the levers. *Voilà!* The latches popped open. As I carefully raised the lid, I was startled to see a virtual treasure trove of jewelry! There were watches, rings and other valuable items, many in boxes or wrapped in special flannel cloth.

"Sir," I said, "there are pieces of jewelry, watches and other beautiful things!"

"Rene," he instructed, "take it and put it in a safe

place. Go to the Ritz tomorrow. The helicopter is going to bring some people to London. I'd like you to go with them, bringing the briefcase with you."

For the rest of the day I worked on making the list, searching through all of Dodi's things and carefully cataloging what I thought would be of interest to his father. I was actually grateful to have something to do, even if it was a rather tedious chore. It gave me a respite from my grief.

But it wasn't until I'd finished the list and flopped down on the living room couch, totally spent, that I made the most amazing and valuable discovery. I was staring at (but not really seeing) the coffee table in front of me with its beautiful display of crystal decanters. I'd handled these decanters countless times when I'd served after-dinner liqueur and brandy to guests. But now there seemed to be something strange about their arrangement. "What is different?" I asked myself. Drawing closer, I realized that there was a shape among them that didn't quite belong there. It was a stray wineglass, camouflaged among the decanters, almost as if someone had hidden it there.

"Who came here?" I wondered, reaching for the glass. Upon closer inspection I could see that it had been hidden away for some time—at least a few days—allowing the last remnants of the wine to crystallize, like fine sugar, at the very bottom. Holding it up to the light, I saw the lipstick imprint and fingerprints left by the lady who had last touched it. Instantly I knew who that was—it was Princess Diana, and this was the glass that she had sipped wine from on the last night of her life.

Carefully, with extreme tenderness, I wrapped the glass in tissue paper and put it in a box. Then I called Mr. Al Fayed again.

"Sir," I said, "I've found the wineglass that the princess used on that final night. I thought you would like to know."

There was a pause, then the weary voice of a grieving father crackled back over the phone lines.

"Did you find a glass for my son, too?" he asked hopefully.

"No, sir," I replied. "When I cleaned up the living room that night, I believe I took his glass away with everything else."

After a whirlwind helicopter ride from Paris to London, I found myself sitting in the waiting area outside of Mr. Al Fayed's Park Lane office, holding both the briefcase and the carefully boxed wineglass on my lap. The secretary led me into his magnificent, well-appointed office. I sat on the fine leather couch in a room that seemed to be completely lined with rich, red-brown wood.

"Wait here," she instructed. "He will come."

Just a few minutes later, Mr. Al Fayed strode into the room, greeting me and shaking my hand warmly. Then he invited me over to a sitting area in his office, where there was a large coffee table surrounded by two sofas and some chairs. We sat facing each other and he immediately asked for the glass. I handed him the box and watched as he carefully opened it, removing it from its nest of tissue paper. He held the glass gingerly, treating it like the precious object it was, and carried it to the window, where he brought it to eye level, slowly rotating it in the sunlight. He stayed there, looking at the glass for a good minute, then sighed heavily and returned to the coffee table.

After he had tenderly packed the glass away in its box, he asked me to open the briefcase. He laid out all the jewelry, examined each piece carefully, and returned everything to the briefcase. When the lid was finally snapped shut and the latches locked, he turned to face me.

"All right, Rene," he said kindly. "Now what do you want to do?"

I knew he was referring to my future. I also had been thinking a great deal about it in the past few days. I was now without a job; my boss was dead. I was going to have to go home and start all over again.

"Mr. Al Fayed," I said, sighing deeply, "all I want to do is leave. I want to go home."

He looked at me and said in an understanding voice, "Rene, go home for two months, take a rest. I would like you to start to work for me when you come back."

I stared at him blankly. I was still in no condition to make any permanent decisions.

"By the way," he asked, "how is your son, Alain?"

He knew that my son was employed at the Ritz, restoring Louis XVI-style furniture.

"He's doing well, sir, thank you very much," I replied. "He still works for you."

"I want to make sure that he is OK. I want you to

know that his place will be secure, and I am going to call Frank Klein and ask him to give your son a raise. I don't want him to need anything."

I was very touched. I stood up, went to him and impulsively took his head between my hands and kissed him on the forehead.

With watery eyes I said, "Thank you, sir. Thank you very much. God bless you."

That night I stayed at Dodi's Park Lane apartment, thinking of other, happier times when we had been there together. The next morning, I received a call from Mr. Al Fayed's office saying that he wanted to see me. I went immediately, and as I made my way down the hallway to his office I saw at least a dozen large framed pictures leaning against the wall. They were individual shots of Princess Diana and of Dodi Fayed, in color, and at least two feet high by one and a half feet wide.

Mr. Al Fayed greeted me and looked at the pictures.

"Rene," he said, "you can have a picture of each; that's for you."

I was absolutely thrilled. They were beautiful pictures, both of them so good-looking and with such happy smiles. These were copies of the pictures that were displayed in the windows of Harrods after the accident. I was terribly touched that Mr. Al Fayed would give me such a wonderful gift, and I knew I would always treasure those pictures.

Before I headed back to Paris, however, I wanted very much to visit Dodi's grave. After working for him, living in his homes and traveling with him for more than seven years, my mind simply couldn't accept the fact that he was really gone forever. I'd had no chance to say good-bye; his body had been transported to London and buried the day the accident had occurred, while I stayed behind in Paris. I needed to experience some sort of closure, to see for myself that he'd been laid to rest. And, of course, I needed to know that everything at the grave site was in order. Even though my boss had passed away, I couldn't seem to stop being his butler.

Accompanied by one of Mr. Al Fayed's assistants, Karen, and Abdu, a cook, I made the thirty-six-mile trek to Brookwood Cemetery in Surrey, not far from the Fayed family home at Oxted. The grave was situated in the middle of a beautiful garden, surrounded by an immaculate lawn and several flowering bushes and trees. A huge marble headstone, some five feet in length, lay flat on the ground, with a simple inscription: DODI. I stared at it for a long time, thinking how strange it was that the only thing we had left of such a warm, caring, vibrant man was a large slab of cold marble. One minute he was here; the next, gone forever.

Karen invited me to sign the condolence book, but I felt so empty I could hardly think. How could I possibly sum up seven years' worth of feelings in a couple of lines? But finally, through my tears, I wrote: "I left my family to follow you, and now you left me. God will be with you." By the time I'd finished writing these lines, I was crying so hard I could write no more, so I just signed my name and hurried away, feeling completely, utterly demolished.

When I got back to Paris, I immediately started

packing my things. I knew I needed to return to Los Angeles as soon as possible to be reunited with my son Bruno and my friends, and try to figure out what to do next. The possibility of working for Mr. Al Fayed was still there, but I really needed time to think.

Once my bags were packed, I said goodbye to the staff and all my Parisian friends. With my airline ticket in hand, I turned my attention to the one last thing I had left to do. Dodi's cherished dogs, Romeo and Shoe, needed to get settled in their new home. Mr. Al Fayed had said, "Rene, take them to Windsor Villa. They have so much space there and they know the place." They'd always loved our trips there and I knew they'd be happy. But I just wanted to watch them run on the grounds one last time before I left, to convince myself that they would be all right. After all, they'd been my companions since I began working for Dodi, and it wasn't easy to let them go. I'd already lost so much.

Philippe and I gathered up all their things—their food, beds and toys—piling them into the Range Rover along with the dogs. Both Romeo and Shoe were excited, as usual, because they knew they'd be going for a romp around the grounds. To them it was just a trip to that beautiful, grassy place where they could be free; but to me it was another sad milestone, another step away from my old life and into my new one. I envied the dogs their ignorance—and the pain it spared them.

Arriving at the Villa, we drove slowly down the driveway, past the beautiful mansion, to the spacious green lawns the size of football fields. As soon as we let the dogs out of the car, they started to race around with more energy than I'd ever seen before. They were leaping and barking in our direction, as if to say, "C'mon! Let's play!" They continued to jump and run around in circles for several minutes before scampering off in search of whatever sights, sounds or smells would delight their senses. They were home—pure and simple. I knew it was right for them, and that they would be safe and content in the care of the Fayed family.

I watched the dogs for a moment more, then looked at Philippe with a smile tinged with sadness.

"OK," I said resignedly. "They're happy here. We can go."

We climbed into the Range Rover and sped away. I didn't look back.

E P I L O G U E

Final Thoughts

Like just about everyone else in the world, I watched the television coverage of the death of Princess Diana and Dodi Fayed for several days after the accident. And although I had been well aware that the princess was an international celebrity, known and loved by millions, I was completely unprepared for the outpouring of emotion surrounding her death. But what the world didn't realize was that a true fairy-tale romance had also been destroyed in that horrific car accident, making the loss even greater.

As I watched the princess' flag-draped coffin move slowly through central London on a horse-drawn gun carriage, I couldn't help but feel that Dodi had been pushed aside. I wished the world had known what I knew, so they could at least join the two lovers together in their minds, as I did in mine. I was amazed at the mountain of flowers left for Diana in front of

Kensington Palace, as well as at the site of the accident. I also knew that thousands of people were standing in line for hours to sign condolence books in England, America, France and other countries. It helped me to see this outpouring of emotion; I felt as if the world were grieving with me. The love they demonstrated for the princess was gratifying.

But I knew that if the public had known Dodi the way I did, they would be mourning for him as well. I was struck by the contrast between how close they were in life and how far apart they were in death, he in Surrey, she at her family estate at Althorp. But I believe that souls have no barriers, no frontiers, so I am sure that they are together.

A great deal of negative publicity has been generated in the months following the tragic death of Dodi Fayed. For me, one of the most disturbing rumors is that he had a cocaine habit. I worked for him for more than seven years, lived with him in his many homes and was present at his parties, so I would certainly have been aware of any drug use. And I can say, unequivocally, that I never saw him under the influence of drugs. He was also very careful about his use of alcohol. While at home, he did not drink during the day, limiting himself to a pre-dinner vodka martini or a glass of wine, and many times he drank no alcohol at all. The "high" he enjoyed most came from being in the company of his friends.

There has also been talk of unpaid bills or irresponsibility in financial matters. I have absolutely no knowledge of this. What I do know is that every time I hired chefs, waiters, musicians or others on Dodi's behalf, and every time I ordered food, decorations or items for his parties, everyone was paid on time and in full. I also know that he was very generous as an employer in both monetary and personal ways, and that I never met anyone who complained about being "stiffed" or otherwise unfairly treated by him. Everything I observed over a seven-year period clearly demonstrated that he was a perfect gentleman in every way.

Many people have asked me if I think that Dodi and Diana really would have married one day. As the only witness to their love affair from start to tragic finish, I believe with all my heart that they would have. They had a deep, powerful connection; they understood each other to the core, partially because their personalities were so well matched, but also because of their unique situations: Both had been extremely privileged and yet both had suffered deeply. I believe they truly treasured each other, their love and their stolen moments of privacy. It's tragic that they were not able to continue the beautiful dream they had created for themselves.

As for me, I am just grateful for the years I was able to spend with Dodi Fayed. I lived in fabulous residences, met famous, exciting people and saw some of the most beautiful places on earth. Through it all, I was treated with great kindness, consideration and generosity. But the most special, most wonderful experience of all was watching the birth and development of a unique and very beautiful love affair. I was honored to have witnessed it and hope that in some small way I contributed to their happiness.

Today, I am back in Los Angeles in the little one-bedroom apartment at the beach where I was living when I met Dodi Fayed. I spend a lot of time watching the waves curl gently into shore and marveling that the sun—so beautiful, red and glowing as it sits perched on the horizon—can suddenly sink into the ocean and vanish in a matter of seconds, very much like life itself.

I also spend a lot of time walking on the beach, watching lovers stroll hand in hand and hearing them squeal with delight as the waves steal up and wrap themselves around their ankles. Lovers always seem fascinated by waves, sunsets and, of course, each other. Once, I caught a glimpse of a tall, blond young woman walking with a darkly handsome man; they were strolling with their arms around each other. My heart stopped for a second. Could it be...no, of course not. But they reminded me of two whose faces were lit up with the same smiles, the same laughter and the same love—but two whose time was cut short before they could experience all that life's richest blessing had to offer.

I will never forget them. I know that as long as there are lovers, sunsets and boats on calm seas, I'll imagine Diana and Dodi, their faces glowing with love and happiness, talking and laughing endlessly into eternity.

Meriden Public Library